ROVER P4

JAMES TAYLOR

AMBERLEY

First published 2023

Amberley Publishing
The Hill, Stroud,
Gloucestershire, GL5 4EP

www.amberley-books.com

ISBN 978 1 3981 1379 4 (print)
ISBN 978 1 3981 1380 0 (ebook)

British Library Cataloguing in Publication Data.
A catalogue record for this book is available from the British Library.

Typeset in 10pt on 13pt Celeste.
Typesetting by SJmagic DESIGN SERVICES, India.
Printed in the UK.

Contents

CHAPTER 1

The P4 in its Time

There are four thoroughly British icons that characterise the 1950s. The first is the Routemaster bus, the second the Austin FX4 taxi, the third a red telephone box, and the fourth is the Rover P4. The first three are all regularly recognised by tourists, but it is probably necessary to have been there to understand how much the Rover symbolised Britain of the 1950s.

Rover had built up a reputation for building 'One of Britain's Fine Cars' in the 1930s, with a well-organised range of models that were designed to appeal to the better-off members of society. While there were cars of similar size and performance from other makers, a Rover was for the bank manager, the doctor, the lawyer, and other professionals who welcomed quality but did not appreciate ostentation. A Rover had a decent turn of speed; a Rover was reliable; but a Rover never stood out as flashy. A Rover perfectly encapsulated 'Britishness'; it led the field but was invariably discreet and only revealed its finer qualities on closer examination.

Those were the qualities that the Rover Company aimed to perpetuate in the new cars it began to design after the end of the Second World War. Though the world in 1945 was a very different place from the world of 1939 when that war had begun, the company's management was sure that there would still be a place for the sort of cars it had been building before.

In that belief, they were right, but there were several new factors in the equation. Not the least among these was that car design had moved on quite dramatically, notably in the USA which had continued to design and build new cars into 1942, two years after British car factories had stopped making cars and filled their assembly halls with aircraft, tanks and other war equipment. Then there was the problem that the British economy had been stretched to breaking-point by the cost of the war, and that the post-war government therefore had to make the earning of revenue from foreign trade a top priority. On top of that, there were shortages of vital materials such as steel and timber, and it was no surprise that the government exercised control over their allocation; manufacturers who failed to export a certain percentage of their production faced the threat of being denied supplies of raw materials.

Rover got back into the car market quite quickly, reviving some of the models from its 1940 range and putting them back into production as a temporary measure while design went ahead on their replacements. It soon became apparent that these old-model types

In 1945, Rover moved out of its old factory in Coventry, which had been heavily bombed in the Blitz in 1940, and into a new one at Solihull that it had been managing for the Air Ministry during the war years. The facade of this building still exists today, within the Land Rover factory.

Rover got back into production in 1946 with cars that it had been making in 1940. This 1947 16-hp Sports Saloon shows the pre-war style with separate running boards and a tall radiator grille.

were going to struggle in export markets, and that something radically new was going to be needed to replace them – and that caused a problem.

Overall responsibility for the design of Rover's cars at the time lay with the company's Chief Engineer, Maurice Wilks. He was not the only Wilks in a senior position: his older

This 1945 scale model captured Maurice Wilks' first ideas on a new post-war saloon. The boxed headlight design would reappear on the early P4 saloons.

brother Spencer (usually known as SB) was Rover's Managing Director and had played a major part in steering the company back to financial health after the Depression years. Maurice Wilks was an innovative engineer, and he was well aware of the new designs appearing in the USA. In fact, the scale mock-up that reflected his first thoughts on a new post-war Rover in 1945 incorporated some of the latest American ideas on styling. He also arranged for the company to buy examples of Buick and Oldsmobile models from the USA for examination – for which he needed special dispensation because the import of foreign cars was banned at the time.

Maurice Wilks also believed that there would be a big customer demand for small economy cars as Britain gradually got back on its feet after the war, and he drew up plans for just such a car. This was known as the M model (M for Miniature) and was a two-seater that drew heavily on the pre-war Fiat 500 Topolino. It was a promising design, but it soon became clear that both at home and overseas, car buyers did not want to be reminded of the hard times they were going through; they wanted full-sized and more stylish cars to express their relief that the war was over and better times were coming.

The need for an export product was pressing, and Maurice Wilks had run into trouble with his designs for a new full-size Rover. What saved the company was his idea of making a civilian equivalent of the wartime Jeep that was firmly slanted towards the needs of agricultural and light industrial users. It used the simplest of steel pressings, had aluminium alloy body panels (the alloy was easier to obtain than steel), and used a new engine that Rover had planned for its post-war cars. Introduced in April 1948, the Land Rover went on to become a worldwide success, and soon took over from cars as Rover's primary product. It also bought the company some time to get its post-war product right.

Rover had been looking at two new pieces of design when the war broke out in 1939. One was that new engine, which would have both four-cylinder and six-cylinder derivatives to replace the existing engines of those types. Its design was characterised by a highly

Above left: Maurice Wilks, Chief Engineer and the man with overall responsibility for the design and development of new Rovers.

Above right: S. B. Wilks was Rover's Managing Director and was very widely respected in the motor industry.

efficient combustion chamber and by inlet valves mounted above that chamber and exhaust valves in its sides. It was the four-cylinder version of this that went on to power the Land Rover. The other was a new chassis frame that used box section side members instead of the open channel type of the 1930s cars to improve rigidity. The principle of box sections was also employed in the Land Rover.

Both of these items were ready and in production by early 1948, but Maurice Wilks did not yet have the modern body design that he wanted for the new post-war full-size Rover saloon. In order to keep Rovers as competitive as he could, he therefore had his designers draw up a new box section car chassis and fit it with one of the new four-cylinder engines and one of the new six-cylinders. To clothe it, he reworked the old pre-war body style, and the new cars were launched as the Rover 60 and Rover 75 in February 1948, those numbers approximating to the output of their engines in brake horsepower.

These cars, known as P3 types for reasons that will be explained later, were only ever intended to be temporary products. Maurice Wilks knew what he wanted by this stage, but his new design was not ready for production. Back in 1945 and 1946, his aim had been to get a modern design into production as quickly as possible, and with that in mind he grafted various designs of full-width front end panels onto the existing pre-war bodyshell. The results were disappointing, to say the least, but some sort of salvation appeared to be at hand after the summer of 1946, when Studebaker in the USA announced their new post-war range of cars for the 1947 season. They were ultra-modern in style – and, most important, one of them was very close in size to the new Rover that Maurice Wilks was trying to design.

Wilks wasted no time and pulled the necessary strings to obtain two examples for Rover to examine. The two cars probably reached Rover in late 1947. One was immediately pulled

Two new Rover engines...

★ *The new Rover cylinder head design, showing the compact high-efficiency combustion space and generous cooling provision.*

IN the new Rover programme, a number of important mechanical advances are concentrated in a simplified range of high quality models : independent front-wheel suspension; a redesigned chassis; and a completely new engine design—the secret of its performance lying in the special cylinder-head construction. **An example of advanced thought in automobile engineering, test results have shown a remarkable improvement in power and economy.**

When Maurice Wilks' plans for an all-new post-war saloon foundered, he combined the new engine and chassis design with a modified pre-war body to make the P3 model. This advertisement shows the centrally mounted lamp that would influence the P4 design.

apart to see what made it tick; the body of the other was removed and put onto a prototype Rover chassis that became an important part of the test programme for Maurice Wilks' new saloon.

It is worth pausing to explain a couple of points here. First, the new Studebakers were quite revolutionary in their appearance because they depended on what is now called a 'three-box' design. Earlier cars had tended to have sloping rear panels, but these had a protruding boot at the back that visually counterbalanced the bonnet. Their shape was the work of industrial designer Raymond Loewy, and had been refined for production by car stylist Virgil Exner. It was so striking at the time that conservative thinkers described it as the 'going-both-ways' look, suggesting that it was impossible to tell which was the front and which was the back! It was also remarkably elegant, and no doubt that was what had caught Maurice Wilks' interest.

The second point to explain is the internal code names that Rover gave to their cars. It looks as if the company's association with wartime products had given them a taste for code names – they had not used them in the 1930s – and when Maurice Wilks had started work on the new post-war saloon he had called it Model P. That P probably stood for Post-war, although nobody knows for certain. As already explained, he called his economy car design Model M, clearly using similar thinking. Model P did not work out as planned, and the pre-war cars that went back into production in 1946 took on the code of P2 (although there is little evidence for this). The hybrid car introduced in 1948 that combined pre-war styling with a new chassis and engine became the P3 – and the new car that Wilks had been trying to design since 1945 logically became the P4.

In an ideal world, the new P4 model would have been manufactured from the start with the same two engines that had gone into the interim P3 model. However, it became clear during the design stages that this was going to be a very heavy car – Rover could not get its weight down to that of the Studebaker – and although the six-cylinder engine would give adequate performance, a four-cylinder model would simply be underpowered. In any case, Rover needed all the four-cylinder engines they could make for the Land Rover, which was proving to be a runaway success. So work went ahead on P4 as a single model with the six-cylinder engine.

There was inevitably a good deal of pressure to get the new model into production as soon as possible. Some other manufacturers had been able to get their new post-war designs ready for the autumn 1948 motor shows in Europe, but Rover had not. It would clearly be undesirable not to have the new model ready in time for the 1949 shows, and Maurice Wilks probably set that as a deadline. In practice, it did not leave enough time for development of the car, and the slow start to production followed by multiple early specification changes are a clear testament to that.

Maurice Wilks had three different scale models made, each with the three-box design derived from the Studebaker and each with its own combination of other features. They were identified by number-plates ROV 500, ROV 501 and ROV 502, the first elements almost certainly indicating 'Rover 1950 model'. A choice of features was made and the project probably proceeded to a full-size mock-up in late 1948; a second such mock-up was made in February 1949, and was badged as a Rover Viking. If there was any serious intention to call the new car that, it was soon abandoned in favour of the 75 name that had been given to its predecessor.

For a time, it looked as if Rover would produce an economy car, but the M model was cancelled before entering production.

Early attempts at a post-war design were not satisfactory. All were based on a pre-war bodyshell to save time and costs, with suggested modifications made from plasticene.

The 1947 Studebakers proved inspirational, and Maurice Wilks bought two examples of the Champion Regal four-door sedan for Rover to examine. (Ken Watkin)

This rear view of a Studebaker shows its most revolutionary feature – a projecting boot that visually balanced the bonnet. (Ken Watkin)

This mock-up was very close to the eventual production design, and incorporated the famous 'Cyclops eye' fog lamp in the middle of a slatted radiator grille. This piece of design was probably inspired by the centrally-positioned but free-standing auxiliary lamp of the P3, although there certainly were precedents elsewhere for a built-in central lamp: the 1948 Tucker Torpedo had one, for example. It has been suggested that the idea came from Studebaker, but in fact their central 'bullet' motif did not appear until their 1950 models were announced in mid-1949.

The first prototype body was then constructed and mounted on a prototype P4 chassis in May or June 1949 – desperately close to the planned introduction of the new model in September and certainly too late for any major changes to be made. It probably already had the Birmabright aluminium alloy boot, bonnet and door panels that helped save weight and would become standard in production. A few details were in fact tidied up, perhaps purely to simplify manufacture, but this was the car that was announced at the 1949 Earl's Court Motor Show as the new Rover 75.

Inevitably, its radical new design upset some of Rover's more conservative customers. It was bad enough that it no longer had a proper radiator grille and a set of running boards, but the obvious American influences in the design were a little too much to take for some people. Rover did gradually tone it down over the next couple of years, and in particular came up with a new radiator grille that more readily recalled the Rover grilles of old. Yet by this stage, other designs in the latest idiom were appearing, and the Rover no longer looked so strange.

By the mid-1950s if not earlier, the P4 had been fully accepted by its target customers. And it was in the mid-1950s that it gained the nickname that has seemed so appropriate for it ever since. It became the 'Auntie' Rover. The name conjured up images of dignified and prim maiden aunts with long, sweeping dresses (like the out-turned lower body sides on the P4

Scale model ROV 500 was photographed against a drawing of the main Rover office building. Note the awkwardly tall bonnet and the headlamps mounted behind glass.

Right: Like ROV 500, ROV 501 had a divided windscreen, and both doors hinged on the centre pillar.

Below: ROV 502 had a series of variations on the same basic design.

itself) and an ultra-conservative approach to life. The car's image is most easily understood by comparing it with the Jaguar saloons that were similar in price. The Jaguar, at the time, was seen as a 'cad's car', and no self-respecting Rover owner would wish to be seen dead in a Jaguar. Similarly, no sporting-minded Jaguar owner would give the staid Rover a second glance. They were poles apart.

In fact, the origin of the 'Auntie' name was more complex. It was dreamt up in 1958 when three motoring journalists borrowed a Rover 90 from the company's press fleet to drive down to Casablanca where they were to report on the Grand Prix. Among them was Ted Eves of *Autocar*, who remembered many years later that the car did not miss a beat throughout their long journey. His colleague Denis Jenkinson (of *Motor Sport*) said that the car looked after them so well that it was all like going to Auntie's for tea – even down to the clock on the walnut mantelpiece – the P4 of course had its clock centrally placed in its wooden dashboard. After that, all 90s were 'Aunties'!

There was a great deal of affection for the P4 within the Rover Company, too. The company's in-house historian wrote a special feature about it in the edition of the company newsletter that followed the end of production in May 1964, giving it the evocative sub-title of 'a tribute to P4 as it slips into the shadows'. By this time, the car was of course distinctly old-fashioned in both looks and engineering, and at Rover it had already been upstaged by the more expensive P5 3-litre and by its own ultra-modern replacement, the P6 2000. Yet above all, the car had engendered a lasting respect among its customers. It was viewed as an embodiment of traditional British values – and even though those took a hammering in the 1960s, the car never lost its image of a solid, dependable machine that was engineered to the very highest standards.

Of course, the P4 went through a period when it was simply an old car, available cheaply and not really worth repairing if something went wrong. Yet surprisingly large numbers remained in good condition and were cherished by their owners. Enthusiastic owners of older Rovers often owned a P4 as an everyday car, recognising the spiritual similarities between them. In 1977, as the classic-car movement was gaining traction in Britain, an owners' club was founded for the P4 range. Today, the Rover P4 Drivers' Guild has members worldwide who appreciate the qualities and the ethos of these lovable old machines that are welcomed at classic car meets everywhere.

HOW MANY WERE THERE?

The Rover 'season' or model year began in September and ended with the annual works holiday the following August. A car built in, for example, September 1949 was a 1950 model, and so on. The dates shown in this book refer to the model year unless otherwise indicated.

In the fifteen years of P4 production, a grand total of 130,342 examples were built. The table that follows shows annual totals of each individual model as well as overall annual totals.

Season	Model	Model total	Annual total	Remarks
1950	75	5,220		including 5 Marauders
		30	5,250	30 2.6 prototypes
1951	75	10,279	10,279	including 10 Marauders
1952	75	5,768	5,768	Short 'season'
1953	75	8,000	8,000	
1954	60	2,181		
	75	4,000		
	90	7,305	13,486	

Season	Model	Model total	Annual total	Remarks
1955	60	1,491		
	75	3,637		
	90	8,280	**13,408**	
1956	60	1,601		
	75	2,740		
	90	8,770	**13,111**	
1957	60	855		
	75	1,137		
	90	3,493		
	105R	1,902		
	105S	1,502	**8,889**	Suez Crisis hit sales
1958	60	1,895		Computed total
	75	1,422		
	90	4,187		
	105R	1,638		Computed total
	105S	3,713	**12,855**	Computed total, 105S
1959	60	1,643		
	75	1,038		
	90	3,868		
	105	2026	**8,575**	
1960	80	3,085		
	100	7,705	**10,790**	
1961	80	1,950		
	100	4,400	**6,350**	
1962	80	865		
	100	4,416	**5,281**	
1963	95	2,413		
	110	2,832	**5,245**	
1964	95	1,267		
	110	1,788	**3,055**	
Grand Total			130,342	

INDIVIDUAL MODEL TOTALS

Model	Seasons	Model Total	Model	Seasons	Model Total
60	1954–59	9,666	**100**	1960–62	16,521
75	1950–59	43,241	**105R**	1957–58	3,540
80	1960–62	5,900	**105S**	1957–58	5,215
90	1954–59	35,903	**105**	1959	2,026
95	1963–64	3,680	**110**	1963–64	4,620

CHAPTER 2

The Early 75, 1950–53

Somehow, Rover overcame all the materials shortages and other difficulties of the time to have no fewer than five new Rover 75s, one in each of the planned colours, ready in time for the Earl's Court Motor Show in September 1949. They were accompanied by a specially prepared chassis that showed the new model's mechanical details, and the one in Pastel Blue – a most attractive colour that Rover probably thought the best of the bunch – was highlighted on a revolving turntable.

The Rover stand at Earl's Court in 1949 featured five examples of the P4 in different colours, plus a bare chassis.

Star of the stand was a Pastel Blue 75 mounted on a turntable. This very early car had not only chromed headlamp surrounds but also chrome trim on the air-intake grilles.

A Pastel Blue car, quite possibly the one from the turntable, also took part in the Lord Mayor's parade in London in September, giving many members of the public their first glimpse of the new Rover. Not everybody was impressed. 'It is not a bit like the old Rover; I don't like it,' wrote the motoring correspondent of the *Bristol Evening World*.

Behind the scenes, Rover were playing catch-up fast. They had been running the first prototype of the P4 for only about three months by the time the first production body shells arrived from Pressed Steel in August to be turned into complete cars. So the development process had not even been completed by the time production began. One result was that production was very slow to build up, and real volume production did not begin before November. Rover deliberately limited it to 100 cars a week at first, in order to conserve supplies of raw materials for Land Rover production, but in practice it would be some months before that figure was reached. By the end of the year, probably no more than 150 or so cars had left the assembly lines.

Not that the customers complained; in Britain at least, they were already accustomed to not being able to buy a new car. The government's insistence on exports meant that only small numbers of new cars were available from any manufacturer, and deserving cases such as doctors were given priority to purchase them. Petrol was still rationed, so there was almost no scope for leisure motoring.

All this provided welcome relief at Rover. The first few months of production brought multiple specification changes on the assembly lines as what was really the development process continued. In these circumstances, Rover was understandably reluctant to release cars to the press, and although the leading weekly motoring magazines were granted brief early drives in cars described as prototypes, no proper press demonstrator would be ready

Underneath the strikingly new body shape was an immensely sturdy chassis with box-section side members.

The six-cylinder engine had twin carburettors and an oil-bath air cleaner. The oil filter was mounted accessibly on the cylinder head, and is visible here as the silver object just beyond the black tubular air-box. Note also the trunking from the wing-mounted air vents; the nearer one fed the footwell vents and the one on the far side fed the heater.

until the end of April 1950 – seven months after the new P4 had been announced. By that time, the specification had settled down a little more.

It took time for the soundness of the P4 design to become appreciated. It was an immensely sturdy car with a high degree of refinement thanks to its rigid box section chassis frame and all-steel body. Its top speed of over 80 mph was excellent for the time, although the car's great weight and taller gearing did make its acceleration less lively than that of the six-cylinder P3 model that it replaced despite a change to twin carburettors. The four-speed gearbox with no synchromesh on the bottom two gears was a tried and tested Rover item, and was allied to a traditional Rover freewheel to give clutch-free gear changing, and overall the driving experience was remarkably refined. The handling was reassuring, although this was not a car that could be hurled about like a sports model. The new 75 preferred to proceed with dignity; it was a Rover, after all.

Controversies

That said, there were plenty of reasons why established Rover customers did not immediately take to it. It did not look like a Rover, with its full-width body and strange front end whose 'Cyclops' fog lamp was embedded in a grille that was not remotely like the traditional Rover type. The earliest cars had chromed headlamp surrounds and chrome frames around the air intake vents below them, and these were seen as vulgar and American. Rover had abandoned both features by January 1950, although the headlamp surrounds remained on cars exported to the USA and on some others.

There were even more controversial features inside the car. The extra body width made possible by the absence of running boards was welcome, but the bench-style front seat that made the car a full six-seater was unfamiliar. So was the gearchange mounted on the steering column that made room for a third passenger in the middle of that seat. Push-button interior door releases instead of handles, and rectangular rather than round instruments, were also unfamiliar, both features inspired directly by the Studebakers that Rover had examined. Then that protruding boot did not offer as much space as it seemed to promise, with a sloping floor to clear the petrol tank and the spare wheel laid in it with little to keep it from soiling luggage. Rover later made a gaiter available to remedy this.

Above left: Pastel Blue was clearly the favoured colour for the new 75, and this is it. These early cars had Lucas 'cat's eye' headlamps.

Above right: Although there were few identifying badges on the car, the Rover name appeared twice at the front.

Above: The 1950 models had rectangular instruments, inspired by the 1947-model Studebakers that Rover had examined.

Left: Also inspired by the Studebaker were press-button interior door releases.

Nevertheless, proper acquaintance with the car revealed its virtues. After trying a prototype in September 1949, *Autocar* magazine reported that this was 'altogether a car of superlative charm'. Its rival, *Motor,* tried the press demonstrator in May 1950 and wrote that it was 'at all times quiet and silky by virtue of an engine of unusual merit'. Rover, meanwhile, were working on several changes to improve its appeal, and the importance of

Above: The Cyclops boot was not trimmed, but simply painted with a black protective compound, and the spare wheel was not ideally placed.

Right: The original interior lights had quite ornate lenses.

The rectangular instruments proved controversial and were replaced on 1951 models by round dials.

the export market was behind a major one in June 1950 when the number of slats in the grille was reduced (from fifteen to eight) to counter overheating at speeds above 70 mph on Continental roads.

For the 1951 season that began in September 1950, there were more big changes. The controversial instruments were replaced by a set of neat round ones that, with minor changes, would see out the life of the car. The electric fuel pump was relocated to reduce noise; an all-hydraulic braking system arrived; and conventional interior door release handles replaced the unloved interior push buttons. Even so, manufacturing shortages were still a fact of life in Britain, and the first 1,330 1951-model cars were built with various hybrid specifications as old-model parts had to be used to keep the assembly lines running while supplies of the new parts became available.

Looking to the Future

These were ambitious times. Rover pressed on with plans for shipping cars abroad as kits of parts for overseas assembly in markets where import taxes were high, but the numbers involved were always small. The only places outside Solihull where these early cars were assembled were Dublin and Bombay. Maurice Wilks also continued to look at ways of reducing the P4's weight, although an experiment with an all-aluminium body shell led nowhere. Nevertheless, his plans to expand the range of P4 models available did bear fruit. On the one hand, he looked at creating a more powerful engine for the car, and on the other he looked at the possibility of two-door variants – a drophead coupé to match those Rover had offered in the late 1930s, and a fixed-head coupé as well. There is more about these experiments in the next chapter.

One of the experimental Siamese-bore 2.6-litre engines shows how it got its name: the cylinders are arranged in pairs, close enough to leave no room for waterways between the pairs. (Colin Blowers)

A 1951-model Cyclops in preservation today. The door mirror was common in export territories, but wing mirrors were generally preferred in Britain.

The sloping boot of the early cars made for an elegant appearance, although it was not very practical, and only Cyclops models had that large opening handle above the number plate. Below the lights are the Rover-approved reflectors, introduced to meet new British lighting requirements from 1954.

Many Cyclops models exported to the USA had a cover over the foglamp with the number '75' punched out of it. This car also has the chromed headlamp panels that were discontinued for most other markets in early 1950.

There were no worthwhile power gains to be made from the existing six-cylinder engine, and so Wilks approved a scheme to enlarge it. Trials of the larger engine in a special group of thirty otherwise standard 1950-model saloons revealed cooling problems, and Wilks had the engine redesigned before approving it for the Rover 90 two years later. These original trials engines were simply big-bore versions of the standard six-cylinder with a 2.6-litre capacity, and the enlarged bores did not leave room for water passages around each cylinder. The cylinders were therefore paired in what was called a 'siamese-bore' arrangement, and it was this that caused the problem. It is something of a miracle that one of these thirty special cars still survives today.

A New Face: The 1952 Models

Arguably, the Cyclops 75s belonged to the period in which Rover was still finessing the P4; in the beginning, development that in easier times might have been done before production began was actually done on the production cars. The initial design was then 'corrected' on the 1951 models, and by this time Maurice Wilks had begun to think about the next stages in the P4's development.

Before any radically new models could enter production, though, there would have to be a further series of 'corrections', and these appeared on the cars introduced for the 1952 season. There was no reason to make changes to the engine, to the gearbox (the column change would do for the moment), or to the recently-introduced round instruments. On the other hand, changes to the appearance were certainly desirable, and these were scooped up in a new specification for the Rover 75 that was actually announced in March 1952 at the Geneva Motor Show. This was late in the season, and in fact the first 1952-model 75s had not left the assembly lines until January while old-model cars were still being made in February.

Exactly why the new models were so late in arriving is less than clear, but the cause was very likely to have been changes to the Land Rover. In autumn 1951, it changed from its original 1.6-litre engine to a 2-litre type, and the addition of major changes to the P4 at the same time would probably have caused more disruption to manufacturing than the company thought was advisable. One result of extending the 1951 season for the P4 was inevitably that build totals went up: in the seventeen months of Rover's '1951', the company built nearly twice as many cars as they had in the twelve months of the 1950 season. Equally inevitably, the build total for just seven months of the 1952 season was correspondingly reduced.

The most obvious new feature for the 1952 models was a new radiator grille, which replaced the slatted Cyclops type with an elegant design that incorporated the traditional Rover triangular model badge at the top and was quite clearly related to the old pre-war design. A bright metal Viking's-head motif on the nose of the bonnet just above it finished the front end off neatly, and the whole design, albeit with minor alterations, was another feature that would see out the production life of the P4. The grille was a complete success, and so much so that AEC copied it for their buses and trucks in 1954; a version of it eventually ended up on the AEC-built Routemaster bus for London Transport that became one of the icons mentioned in the last chapter.

A thorough overhaul of the heating and ventilating system did away with the air intakes below the headlights and replaced them with a scoop-type ventilator at the base of the windscreen that could be opened or closed from inside the car. This fed air to a more powerful heater. There had been major work at the back of the car, too, where the spare

LWD 787 was a press demonstrator of the 1952-season Rover 75. The new grille is clear in this picture, and just visible at the base of the windscreen is the new hinged air scoop, which is partially open here. Lucas 'tripod' headlamps were now standard.

The 1952 models brought revised boot arrangements, with the spare wheel under the boot floor (and a reshaped petrol tank to suit). The tail lights now have painted bodies with chromed rims, and the rear window has been widened.

wheel was relocated in its own compartment below the boot floor. A wider rear window gave a better view out of the back of the car, while a recessed front seat back provided more rear-seat legroom and a reserve fuel switch replaced the low-fuel warning light of the Cyclops.

Probably most important was a major improvement in refinement through the use of new Silentbloc rubber mountings between body and chassis and on the road springs, which reduced the amount of road noise that was transmitted into the bodyshell. This new model was, said *Motor* magazine, 'a car for which admiration slowly but very surely increases as substantial numbers of miles roll inconspicuously by'. Unfortunately, it was around 100 lb heavier than the Cyclops models it replaced, and the last thing the P4 needed was extra weight. Both in-gear acceleration times and fuel consumption suffered as a result.

PERFORMANCE FIGURES

Rover claimed the following performance figures for the early P4 models. The difference between those for the 1950–1951 Cyclops and the 1952–1953 cars can only be attributed to the extra weight of the later models. The dates are those of the relevant Technical Details booklet that was issued to sales staff.

Date	Dry Weight	Top Speed	Fuel Consumption
November 1949	3,083 lb	80 mph	24–28 mpg
January 1952	3,200 lb	80 mph	22–26 mpg

Minor Changes: The 1953 Models

There was no need to make further changes for the 1953 season that began that autumn, although Rover did introduce some new paint colours, and also made available the first P4s with two-tone paintwork, which had been tried experimentally on some of the thirty test cars with 2.6-litre engines in 1951. Two schemes were available – two-tone green and two-tone grey – and the darker shade covered the roof panel only. Just one mid-season change followed, when the Panhard rod on the rear axle was deleted on production and, as Rover had determined that it served no good purpose, a service recommendation went out to remove it from existing cars as well.

One very encouraging new trend became apparent during the 1953 season, and that was a major upturn in sales on the home market. This was not so much triggered by Rover making better cars as by the British government relaxing many of the restrictions that had favoured exports over home sales. From this point on, exports of the P4 would gradually decline, but overall sales would remain at satisfactory levels for many more years.

Four on the Floor

Not everybody liked the column-mounted gearchange of the early 75s, and J. W. Gethin's, the Rover distributors at Tyseley, near Birmingham, had clearly received their fair share of customer grumbles about it. By 1953, and possibly as early as 1952, they had developed a floor-change conversion. The design was almost certainly by Peter Wilks, who was at the time running the Gethin's service department after the failure of his Marauder car company (see Chapter 3).

'This conversion has been developed for many owners of the new 75 who still prefer the original type of gear change,' read the advertising leaflet. In practice, it used components of the gearchange of the 1948–49 Rover P3 models, with the lever offset to the driver's side by 6 inches from the centre of the car. Early versions used the straight gear lever of the P3, but later ones added a cranked extension, though leaving the reverse détente button at the top of the main lever.

The conversion could be done by Gethin's themselves or could be bought as a kit of parts. It was never very common.

The Gethin's gearchange conversion is seen here on a 1953 75. (Gary Nelson)

CHAPTER 3

Pushing the Boundaries

The huge difficulties that faced car manufacturers in Britain in the late 1940s and early 1950s did not prevent the more far-sighted of them from planning for the return of more normal times. At Rover, Maurice Wilks certainly did have one eye trained optimistically on more favourable trading conditions, and as soon as the new Rover 75 was successfully introduced to the public, he began looking at how the Rover P4 range could be further developed. He was not alone in this, either: three of his engineers had their own views about how the P4 could make the basis of a sports car, and they set up in business to produce exactly that.

By 1950, Maurice Wilks was thinking not only of a more powerful P4, as explained in the last chapter. He was also thinking about two-door drophead and fixed-head coupé derivatives of the car. Some of the inspiration for those came from experiments with gas turbine engines, for which a modified P4 was used as the host vehicle. And not least of the further options he entertained was to use a shortened P4 chassis as the basis of a rugged estate car that would be part-Rover and part-Land Rover.

JET 1 – The Gas Turbine Pioneer

Chronologically, the earliest of these endeavours to use the P4 as the basis of something else was the gas turbine programme. Experimental P4s with gas turbine engines were built over a period of four years from 1950, and one of them became very famous indeed when it demonstrated its high-speed potential during some test runs in 1952. First, however, it is important to explain how and why Rover became involved with gas turbine propulsion.

When war broke out in 1939, Frank Whittle was working on the development of a jet engine. The Air Ministry took a keen interest in this, and in 1941 arranged for Rover engineers, led by Maurice Wilks, to assist Whittle's team. Although the two parties fell out and the jet engine work was transferred to Rolls-Royce in 1943, Wilks retained a keen interest in the ideas he had encountered. After the war, he established a special department at Rover to look into using the principles of jet propulsion to produce an engine that could power a road car.

This engine was known as a gas turbine type rather than a jet engine. It was not designed to produce thrust like an aircraft engine, but it used the same combustion

Above: JET 1, the world's first gas turbine car, was built on a P4 chassis by Tickford, using several body panels from the then current 75 Cyclops.

Left: JET 1 was awarded the RAC's Dewar Trophy for outstanding achievement in the automotive world.

principles to provide power that was harnessed mechanically to drive the road wheels. By 1949, the Rover team had developed a viable engine, and was ready to try it out in a prototype car.

The simplest solution was to put the gas turbine engine into a car that was already in production and readily available, and so a P4 chassis and body were adapted for the purpose. The major problem was the large volume of exhaust produced by the gas turbine engine, and Rover decided to put the engine behind the driving compartment so that its exhaust could vent to air behind the car's occupants. This solution precluded the use of a closed saloon body, and so a standard P4 body was passed to coachbuilders Tickford of Newport Pagnell for conversion into an open two-seater.

The car first ran in March 1950 with a 100-bhp gas turbine engine and demonstrated its ability to reach speeds of 85 mph – more than the standard petrol-engined Rover 75 could achieve. A couple of months after that, Rover managed to obtain the registration number JET 1 for it, and the car has been known by that name ever since (although its actual identification number is XT1 – experimental Turbine number 1).

Over the next two years, further work on the engine produced a much more powerful design with 230 bhp. Maurice Wilks was well aware of the publicity that followed high-speed record runs, and he now suggested taking JET 1 to the newly opened Jabbeke highway in Belgium to do some maximum-speed testing. Jabbeke was already established as a venue for such events and had been used (with the co-operation of the Belgian Gendarmerie) by Jaguar; Triumph would follow in 1953.

Spen King, who was now running Rover's gas turbine department, prepared the car by taking a lot of weight out of it. He also redesigned its nose with a more aerodynamic shape that reflected the latest 1952-model P4 front end and, for safety, he persuaded Dunlop to provide a set of four of their experimental disc brakes: the all-round drum brakes of the standard Rover 75 were certainly not going to cope with stopping from the speeds that everybody anticipated.

The Jabbeke highway was booked for two days in June 1952, and a team of Rover engineers went there with the car. The first runs were made with King's cousin Peter Wilks in the driving seat; overnight, adjustments were made and on the second day, King himself drove JET 1 to a maximum speed of over 152 mph. Rover got the publicity they wanted.

This was not the last of Rover's experiments with a gas turbine car, but JET 1 had proved its point. Rover handed it over to the Science Museum in London in 1958 for permanent exhibition, and it is still there.

Meanwhile, in the period after JET 1's first public appearance in 1950, Rover began to look at a more practical gas turbine car that could realistically be produced for sale to the public.

Once again, they used a P4 as its basis. By mid-February 1951, the plan was to mount the gas turbine engine under the bonnet of a standard P4 saloon and to take its exhaust out to the rear through the side members of the chassis. This involved a major redesign with much deeper chassis side members, and the car known as T2 took to the road in March 1952. It worked – but only to a point. Unburnt paraffin tended to collect in the side members and then ignite. Extensive lagging reduced the fire risk, but it was clear that this approach to a gas turbine car was impracticable.

Above: A more streamlined front end was designed for the record attempts at Jabbeke, and the car survives in this form today.

Left: A later model P4 saloon became T2A, with its engine in the back and a huge exhaust funnel above it.

Undaunted, Spen King and team decided to relocate the engine in the boot of the car, with a large funnel in place of the boot lid to take the exhaust gases out at roof height. T2 may have been based on a Cyclops model, but its rear-engined T2A successor had the new front end of the 1954 models. It first ran in 1954, but was not very successful. Spen King decided that the next step would have to be to design a special gas turbine car and not to try adapting existing production models. There would be no more gas turbine P4s.

Dropheads and a Coupé: The Tickford Cars

Before the Second World War, the Rover range had been much wider than it had become in the post-war austerity years. The Rover 75 P4 was available only as a saloon and only with one size of engine; in the pre-war years, Rover had offered a range of cars with five different engine sizes and with saloon, sports saloon, coupé and drophead coupé bodies. Although the distinction between saloon and sports saloon had subsequently become irrelevant (by pre-war definitions, the four-window configuration of the P4 made it a sports saloon), Maurice Wilks clearly believed that there was scope for coupé and drophead coupé bodies in the P4 range. The good looks of the two-door JET 1 gas turbine car must have been a factor in his decision to investigate the possibilities further.

Above: Tickford were called upon to create a pair of drophead coupés based on Cyclops models. This was the first one and went to the MP for Solihull.

Right: The second car was painted Pastel Blue and has been painstakingly restored to original condition. (Steve Glover, CC BY 2.0)

Only two pictures are known of the Tickford-bodied coupé. On the original of this one, it is possible to see that the car had a wide, three-piece rear window – the precursor of the design adopted on mainstream saloons for 1955. (David Boar)

Impressed by what the coachbuilder Tickford had achieved for that car, Maurice Wilks asked that company to build a pair of drophead coupé bodies on the standard Rover 75 chassis, and to add to these a single prototype of a fixed-head coupé using the same basic design. The first drophead was completed in 1950 and the other two cars by summer of 1951; they were evaluated by Rover, but no production followed. Wilks had had another idea, which was to get an Italian coachbuilder to produce a more glamorous and exciting pair of designs. The three experimental Tickford cars were sold off to the public; two have disappeared, but one of the dropheads still survives today and is a fascinating reminder of what might have been.

Dropheads and a Coupé: the Pinin Farina Cars

In the post-war years, Italian coachbuilders were making waves with new and attractive designs, and among them was the Pinin Farina company of Turin. Battista Farina – 'Pinin' was the nickname for the youngest member of the family – had learned the coachbuilding trade at his older brother's company, Stabilimenti Farina, and set up on his own in 1930. During the ensuing decade, he had developed a reputation as the most progressive of the Italian coachbuilders, and after the war he quickly re-established his claim to that title. His creations caught Maurice Wilks' eye.

By late November 1951, Wilks had arranged with Pinin Farina for the Italian company to build a convertible body to their own design on a P4 chassis. The chassis itself was shipped to Italy in February 1952, and appears not to have returned to Solihull until summer 1953, by which time it was carrying an extraordinarily attractive convertible body finished in metallic gold with a red soft-top and beige seats. Unsurprisingly, its overall lines were similar to those of some other Pinin Farina designs of the time, but the Rover nevertheless had some unique features.

Some of its features would never have made a production model, of course. Rover liked wooden dashboards, and that of the Pinin Farina car was in metal, painted to match the body. But a particularly striking feature was a wide, recessed version of the new Rover

Above: The Pinin Farina drophead coupé was painted in a striking colour scheme. Both this car and the Mulliner copy still survive.

Right: The company was still called Pinin Farina when the Rovers were built, but was already using a badge that combined the two words.

grille that harmonised perfectly with the lines of the car. It would be influential, too: there is no doubt that it inspired later Rover production designs for the P5 3-litre and for the P4 itself. Rover management were sufficiently impressed with the whole car to display it on their stand at the Earl's Court Motor Show in October 1953 alongside the new P4 production models described in the next chapter.

It was a huge hit: *The Motor* described it as 'beautifully proportioned' with 'unmistakable Rover characteristics ... blended perfectly with a body that combines dignity, elegance and practical comfort.' Maurice Wilks clearly intended to take things further, and in the months after the show he not only commissioned Pinin Farina to build a fixed-head version of the car, but also asked coachbuilder Mulliner's of Bordesley Green to build a 'production prototype' – a replica of the car that would also provide data to help turn the hand-built prototype into a low-volume production car. Both were built on 1954-model Rover 90 chassis.

Two things conspired to prevent the project going any further. One was that Bertie Henly of Rover's London distributors had concerns about refinement issues in a convertible Rover and flatly refused to sell one; the other was that Mulliners, who had built the production prototype, signed a contract in June 1954 to work exclusively for Standard-Triumph. There may have been a third factor: demand for Land Rovers continued to increase and Rover had to keep finding new resources to build enough to meet it.

So all three cars were sold to the public. The fixed-head car went to Spain, was converted to left-hand drive, and was written off in an accident. The two convertibles both survive today after sympathetic restoration and are regularly seen at classic car events – they look as good as ever.

The fixed-head coupé by Pinin Farina was another superb concept, and some elements went on to inspire the design of Rover's P5 3-litre.

Neither One Thing nor the Other: The Road-Rover

The Land Rover proved a huge international success from the moment it was launched in 1948, but attempts to sell a seven-seat Station Wagon (with coach built body by Tickford) foundered on cost. The hand-built body made the Station Wagon far more expensive than the standard utility model, and as a passenger-carrying vehicle it was subject in Britain to Purchase Tax, from which the utility models were exempt as commercial vehicles. An increase in that tax in the April 1951 Budget was probably the last straw, and Rover withdrew the model that summer.

Nevertheless, Maurice Wilks was convinced that there would be customers for a rugged estate-car type of vehicle, and he determined to base it on a shortened P4 car chassis with a utilitarian body that would be simple and relatively cheap to make. Initially known as the Utility Car during 1951, it subsequently became known as the Road-Rover.

Right: The Road-Rover was a boxy estate car built on a shortened P4 chassis. This is the final Series I car, which still survives.

Below: The chassis of a Series II Road-Rover shows its clear relationship to the P4. It has a 2.0-litre four-cylinder engine, as used in the Rover 60.

The transatlantic looks of the Series II Road-Rover were distinctly controversial.

The first prototype was built on the chassis of a 1952-model P4, with its wheelbase shortened to 97 inches, and was probably powered by the Land Rover version of the 2-litre four-cylinder engine. By April 1953, six broadly similar prototypes were running, and SB Wilks formally proposed to the Rover Board to put it into production. More prototypes were built as new ideas entered the equation, but Maurice Wilks was by this time too busy on more pressing matters to run the project effectively, and the last of twelve cars was put on the road in June 1955.

The whole project was re-evaluated during 1956, and Wilks gave the project to his newly appointed Chief Engineer (Cars). Wilks himself probably designed the ungainly new body that resembled a shrunken Chevrolet station wagon, and more prototypes followed. Production was scheduled and put back several times, and three pilot-production cars were built in November 1958, but by April 1959 the project was dead, squeezed out of the schedule because Rover had too many other projects to deal with at the time. Two of these second-series prototypes still survive, as does one of the first-series cars.

The Marauder

The good performance and handling qualities of the Rover 75 were not lost on some of Rover's younger engineers, who drew up plans in 1949 to build a three-seater sports derivative on a modified chassis. George Mackie, Peter Wilks, and Spen King (the latter two both nephews of the Wilks brothers) called their car the Marauder, and Mackie and Wilks left Rover to make it, establishing their own company to do so. King put money into the project, but stayed at Rover.

A first prototype was built in 1950, on a shortened chassis with the engine relocated further back to improve handling, some suspension and steering changes, and a body constructed by Dorridge coachbuilder Richard Mead that deliberately echoed some of the P4's lines. Press reaction was quite enthusiastic, and with the active support of Bernard Willmott, who ran the Rover dealership in Bognor Regis and regularly entered trials and rallies with examples of the marque, the first orders began to arrive.

Five Marauders were built on 1950-model chassis, and their makers developed additional options, including a 100-bhp big-bore 2.4-litre engine and a triple-carburettor installation. However, the Marauder was already an expensive car and could not compete on price or performance with the Jaguar XK120 that was the sports car sensation of the time. In April 1951, the major increase in Purchase Tax inflated its cost in Britain to completely unrealistic levels, and the orders began to dry up.

Later in 1951, a left-hand-drive demonstrator was built in the hope of obtaining sales in Europe, and body production was transferred from Richard Mead to Abbey Panels in Coventry. Ten Marauders in all were built on 1951-model Rover chassis but the last complete car was delivered in April 1952 with a unique fixed-head body. Recognising that sales prospects were not going to improve, the partners decided to dissolve the Marauder Car Company. George Mackie returned to Rover, where he later became head of the Land Rover Special Projects department, and Peter Wilks spent some time with Rover dealers Gethin's in Tysley before rejoining Rover. He took over as the company's Chief Engineer in 1964.

Above: The Marauder again used a shortened P4 chassis, and the outswept skirt panels emphasised its relationship to the Rover saloon.

Right: Just one Marauder was completed with enclosed bodywork, and it still survives today.

CHAPTER 4

New Models, New Look, 1954–56

The 1952 and 1953 models of the Rover 75 had established a satisfactory specification for the P4 range that needed no immediate updates. Nevertheless, Maurice Wilks had been looking at future extensions of the range for some time, and by the autumn of 1953, he had them ready.

By this time, post-war austerity conditions had largely eased in Britain, and this created the market conditions suitable for a wider range of P4s. In fact, the 1954 season would be the first one in which home market sales of the P4 range exceeded export sales. Meanwhile, Land Rover sales showed no signs of slowing down worldwide, and work had been going ahead to develop new and larger versions of the existing model. Rover had enough confidence to put these into production (as the 86-inch and 107-inch models, with a Station Wagon derivative of the short-wheelbase type) at the same time as two new P4 variants and a series of revisions that affected all the 1954-model P4s.

The two new models were the Rover 60 and Rover 90, and they bracketed the existing Rover 75. The 60 was an entry-level car, with a 2-litre four-cylinder engine that promised the 60 bhp its name suggested; the 90 was a new top model, with a 2.6-litre six-cylinder engine delivering 90 bhp. Both these new engines had a 'spread-bore' design with the cylinder bores spread evenly along the length of the cylinder block to give water between all of them. The 75, meanwhile, continued with its earlier narrow-bore engine, which of course had always had water between all the bores.

The two new models were only part of the story, however. For the 1954 season, there were multiple changes to the gearbox and its controls, to the handbrake, and to the appearance of the cars. The gearbox retained the same internal ratios as before, but now came with synchromesh on second gear, leaving only bottom gear unsynchronised. As a freewheel was still standard, the 'crash' first gear presented no real difficulty to even the clumsiest driver. Gear selection was now much easier, too, thanks to a floor-mounted gear lever that had been carefully designed to leave room for the legs of a middle passenger on the bench front seat. This was a quite ingenious device, with a long, cranked lever that earned it the nickname of the 'mustard spoon' from Rover engineers, and it was adjustable to suit the driver.

ROVER
One of Britain's Fine Cars

Artwork tended to make the cars look sleeker than they really were, and the cover of this 1954 season catalogue is no exception. The car illustrates one of the early two-tone colour schemes, with the contrast colour applied only to the roof.

The column gearchange of the earlier cars had not been the only controversial driving control; there had also been criticism of the handbrake, which was positioned where it could give the driver a nasty crack on the knee as he or she got into the car. So for the 1954 models, Rover moved it to a position between the seat and the door. Unfortunately, the customers did not take to this, either. The first versions of the handle were painted black and proved difficult for some drivers to reach. Rover raised the end of the handle by an inch and a half to improve accessibility, but the customers were still not satisfied. A chromium-plated lever followed in April 1954, but that did not meet with approval either, and for the 1955 season the handbrake returned to its original position, albeit with minor changes.

The most obvious change to the appearance of the 1954 cars resulted from a gradual increase in the popularity at home and abroad of flashing turn indicators. The Rovers did not get them yet, but in preparation for their eventual fitting the sidelights were moved from the noses of the front wings into chromed 'torpedoes' on the wing tops. The redundant sidelight apertures remained in the front wings and for most markets were filled by white reflector discs as a temporary measure. Nevertheless, they were filled by flashers on some export models (when two bulbs were fitted in the rear lights to give a red flasher). Few cars now survive with the standard configuration, which lasted only for one year; owners have generally chosen to fit flashing indicators, which are certainly safer than semaphore arms in today's traffic conditions.

The 1954 models had the handbrake located alongside the driver's seat. This one is missing the rubber gaiter at its base; a chromed version of the lever replaced it later in the season. To make room for the handbrake, the door pocket was omitted on this side, although the opposite side had one. (Matt White)

The new gear lever was often known as the 'mustard spoon' for obvious reasons! Very early examples had a more curved lever than the one seen here on a 1955 model, by which time the handbrake had regained its original position.

Just as the 75 had a triangular grille badge bearing its model name, so did the 60 and the 90. However, there were some extra additions to help the top-model 90 stand out from the others. It carried discreet but readily visible chromed script badges that read 'Rover 90' on each side of its bonnet and on the boot lid. It also came with a single Lucas SFT700 fog lamp mounted to the bumper valance on the kerb side of the car.

The 90 was an immediate success, and became by far the best-selling Rover P4 in its first season. Customers valued its acceleration, and although its top speed of 82 mph was not that much higher than could be had from a 75, optional taller (3.9:1) axle gearing available from March 1954 did allow a maximum of 85 mph without doing too much harm to acceleration times through the gears. *The Autocar* tried examples with both gearing options, and concluded that, 'the Rover 90 is a quality car in a class by itself, possibly unique in what it gives, all told, at its price … [it is] very flexible and pleasant at low speeds [and] can be treated very much as a top gear car'. As for the new gear lever, it was 'positive and light in operation and has just about the right movement from gear to gear'. *The Autocar* testers liked the relocated handbrake, but their rivals at *The Motor* offered the criticism that 'a minor drawback is that the driver's side arm-rest offers some obstruction to quick access'.

The 60 was the slowest seller for the 1954 season, and that was no surprise, but it was certainly not an also-ran. *The Motor* described it as 'a most lively performer and in no

Right: With the 1954 models came three matching versions of the latest Rover grille badge, beautifully enamelled on a metal backing plate. This is the one for the 60…

Below left: …this is the one for the middle-of-the-range 75…

Below right: …and this is the one for the 90. The Viking's head mascot was affectionately known within Rover as 'George'.

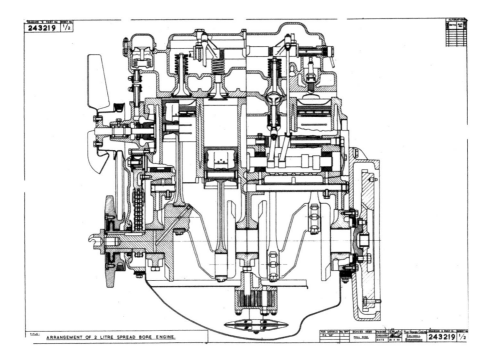

The four-cylinder engine in the 60 was always a spread-bore type, as illustrated in this drawing.

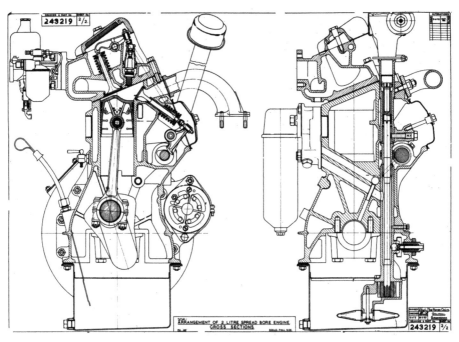

Cross-sections from the front (left) and rear (right) show the layout of the spread-bore engine. The positions of the carburettor, starter motor and paper-element oil filter are immediately obvious.

This 1954 car shows the unique front lighting arrangements for that year. The headlamps were Lucas tripod types, there was a sidelight perched on top of the wing; and the earlier sidelight hole in the wing was filled with a white reflector.

sense a dull utility edition ... a most likeable car which cannot fail to produce an extremely satisfying impression on discerning drivers.' It had the benefit of near-neutral steering characteristics, where the 75 and 90 were prone to understeer. *The Autocar* summed it up by saying that it was 'very much a true quality car, giving with the economy and simplicity of a four-cylinder engine the refinements of bodywork and of detail equipment that are part and parcel of a Rover'.

PERFORMANCE FIGURES

Rover provided the following figures for the 1954 cars to their salesmen. Road tests did not always match them, but the 'official' figures were certainly not wildly inaccurate.

	60	75	90 (4.3 axle)	90 (3.9 axle)
0–50 mph	18.0 sec	16.0 sec	13.5 sec	13.5 sec
0–60 mph	26.0 sec	23.0 sec	19.0 sec	19.0 sec
Max speed	75 mph	80 mph	82 mph	85 mph
Fuel cons	27–30 mpg	24–27 mpg	20–23 mpg	22–25 mpg

A Professional and a Restyle

It is hard not to get the impression that Maurice Wilks was not at his happiest when dealing with car styling. His pre-war designs had been unquestionably elegant, but he had struggled to get to grips with the new trends that were becoming dominant in the immediate post-war years. His solution for the P4 had been to draw quite heavily on the Raymond Loewy Studebaker, but when he needed to design an open two-door derivative of it for the JET 1 gas turbine car, he passed the job to Tickford. When he wanted two-door drophead and fixed-head coupé designs not long afterwards, he again turned to Tickford. Then, sensing the need for something different, he asked Pinin Farina to come up with proposals for the two-door cars.

Wilks also had far more work than he could comfortably cope with by the early 1950s. The need to design and develop new variants of the Land Rover, the need to expand the P4 saloon range, and the need to develop an engine strategy that would suit both products was quite enough for any Chief Engineer to be dealing with at any one time. Styling was one job he could well do without, and by 1953 he had decided that he needed to take on a trained car stylist to deal with the job for him.

The man he recruited was David Bache, who had done an engineering apprenticeship with Austin towards the end of the war and had elected to join the Austin Styling Department under Dick Burzi. Bache joined Rover as its first stylist in August 1953, bringing with him new techniques (such as the use of clay for mock-ups) that he had learned from American stylists working with Austin. Maurice Wilks almost immediately set him to work on some revisions for the 1955-model P4s. Key among them was a new and larger boot.

Although his efforts were quite tightly controlled by Wilks, Bache came up with a masterful set of revisions for the P4. He raised the line of the rear wings and boot lid, creating a much deeper boot space, and at the same time he enlarged the rear window so that it wrapped around the rear body pillars to create a much lighter interior. The three-piece design he adopted was almost certainly inspired by the similar one for the 1951 Tickford fixed-head coupé; the glass was made in three sections because the technology did not then exist to make such a large and complex window as a single item.

An additional requirement was to modify the rear light units. On the one hand, the increasing popularity of flashing turn indicators meant that the P4 would need proper provision for these. On the other, there was the imperative of new lighting legislation in Britain that would come into effect on 1 October 1954. Among the new requirements was for a red reflector on each side at the rear (and this was made retrospective, so Rover provided a kit of parts for earlier P4s). Bache probably did not design the neat vertical lamps he adopted for the 1955 models; more likely is that they came from a catalogue of options designed by Lucas, who made them for other cars as well as the Rover. Nevertheless, they fitted very well into the new rear-end design, and on 1955 cars were matched by clear-lens front indicators in place of the white reflectors of the 1954 models.

Few people realise that Bache did not stop there. He redesigned the front end of the car with raised wing lines to match the rear and a different, neat arrangement of sidelights and indicator flashers that drew on the Lucas catalogue. However, Rover's resources were not infinite, and the decision was taken to spread the cost of the changes by introducing the new rear end for the 1955 season and following up with the new front end for the 1957 season.

So the 1955 and 1956 P4 models all had an interesting hybrid body style with the early boxed-headlight front end allied to the smart new rear end. The slots in the window pillars for semaphore turn signals were simply covered by blanking plates. The range consisted of the same three models as before – four-cylinder 60, and six-cylinder 75 and 90 – and they proved eminently satisfactory. As a result, there were no major changes during the 1955 season.

There was one more important change to the 1955 range, and this one affected the mid-range 75 only. The 2,103-cc six-cylinder engine it had inherited from the P3 75 was by mid-1954

Right: Vokes paper-element air cleaners located on top of the engine began to replace the oil-bath type from the start of the 1954 season. One is just visible on this 1955-season 75 engine – the first of the short-stroke types.

Below: For the 1955 models the boot was enlarged and a new three-piece rear window was introduced. Nevertheless, as seen here, the earlier front end style remained in place, with sidelights mounted on top of the wings.

an odd man out in the Rover range, as it had the original cylinder bore spacing; both the four-cylinder 60 and the six-cylinder 90 now had redesigned 'spread-bore' blocks. So to simplify manufacturing, a new 75 engine was created as a short-stroke version of the 90 engine.

The swept volume worked out at 2,230 cc, and the new engine developed 80 bhp (as compared to the earlier engine's 75 bhp) with a single carburettor instead of the twin installation on the older engine. This of course reduced manufacturing costs and also eliminated the need for tuning the twin SUs. Maximum torque was broadly similar to that of the earlier 75 engine, but a further advantage was that it was developed lower down the rev range than before. Rover quoted improved acceleration of 0–60 mph in 20 seconds, though with slightly worse fuel consumption of 23–26 mpg.

Overdrive and Servo Brakes

The 1956 season brought some more important changes. The Rover engineers were already contemplating P4 models with even higher performance, and with that they were going to need more powerful brakes. The existing all-round drums were sound enough, but there was no doubt they were marginal in a 90 running at full speed, especially if the freewheel was disengaged so that there was no engine braking effect.

Specially painted and partially sectioned, this 90 display chassis is a 1956 model with servo-assisted brakes and overdrive. The vacuum reservoir is clearly visible behind the bumper, and the servo itself is behind the support for the air filter – an oil-bath type normally seen only on export models.

The 90 always had a single fog light in this period, and here it is on a 1956 model with one of the two-tone paint schemes. Semaphore trafficators have gone, to be replaced by flashers; note the domed amber lens on each front wing.

The solution was to add a vacuum servo (made by Clayton-Dewandre) to the 90 and to improve its front brakes as well. This gave the necessary extra stopping power, but the servo could not be used with the freewheel transmission. It depended on vacuum created by the engine, and there was a risk that if an engine stalled at high speed and the car was freewheeling, the servo would be inoperative and there would still be no engine braking.

The answer to that problem was to replace the freewheel by an overdrive. This was geared higher than the standard top gear, so reducing engine revs at high speed, but retained a positive link between engine and rear axle so that engine braking would always be available. The unit chosen was a Laycock De Normanville type, with an electrical control system that allowed automatic engagement and disengagement through a master switch on the steering column.

The result was very successful. *The Motor* said that the overdrive-equipped car was even more effortless than the 90 it had tested earlier with the tall 3.9:1 axle gearing, and that 'speeds of around 80 mph in overdrive (approximately 3,500 rpm) were held for miles on end on various occasions with no sign or sound of effort.' The magazine recorded a top speed of nearly 90 mph. The new brakes 'represent an undoubted improvement and no trace of fade was experienced, whilst the very light but progressive pedal effort was a welcome feature.'

These were not the only improvements for the 1956 season, of course. The 90 actually had a slightly more powerful engine than before, thanks to a raised compression ratio that was feasible now that better-quality petrol was becoming available around the world. All three models now came as standard with pleated leather upholstery that was both more attractive and hard-wearing than the earlier plain leather, and individual front seats became an extra-cost alternative to the standard bench. At the front, amber lenses now replaced the clear-glass indicators at the front, and Rover recommended using them to replace the 1955 type, too.

Few changes were made during the 1956 season, although the overdrive proved so popular on the 90 that Rover made a conversion kit available in March 1956 so that it could be fitted to older 90 models. Right at the end of the season, in summer 1956, the Suez Crisis threatened to bring an increase in petrol prices, and sales of large and thirsty cars such as Rovers slowed right down. As a result, Rover were left with overstocks of 1956-specification cars just as they were about to introduce the visually very different 1957 models. The solution for the home market was to re-equip 154 cars to the 1957 specification and to renumber them as 1957 models – so some early 1957 models are not quite what they seem!

A bench front seat was still standard, but for 1956 the original plain leather upholstery gave way to this more elegant and luxurious-looking pleated style.

CHAPTER 5

Range Expansion, 1957–59

Seven years into its production run, the P4 was by most standards quite an old design, and its separate-chassis construction marked it out as such. Yet there was no sign of its appeal waning, and to help sales along Rover gave the whole range a facelift at the Motor Show in October 1956. On top of that, the range was extended upwards, with two new and more expensive variants.

The 1957-season facelift was the second half of David Bache's mid-decade restyle, and brought the front end changes that he had always intended should go with the larger boot and modified rear end. The front ends of the wings now lost the box shapes around the headlamps, and their crown line was raised as well. Flasher lamps and sidelights were recessed into their faces, and little chromed 'pips' just above the headlights caught the reflection of the side lights and reassured the driver that they were working. This was a

Individual front seats became available on the new 105S and 105R De Luxe models. They were standard on the new 105S and 105R models but cost extra on the others.

typical piece of Rover detail, in this case not the work of the Styling Department but an idea that came from Jim Shaw, the engineer then running P4 development.

The 90 lost its distinguishing foglamp for 1957, probably to help distance it from the two new models, and the popular overdrive now became standard, although a few customers still ordered their 90s with a freewheel. The freewheel did not disappear from the range altogether, and remained standard on the 60 and 75 models for the time being.

The big news for 1957 was the two new models, of course, and these were the 105R and 105S. It looks very much as if they had come about after Rover began investigating the possibilities of an automatic gearbox, which was of course a rarity in Britain in the mid-1950s. Jaguar and Rolls-Royce had both offered American-made automatic gearboxes as an option from 1952, mainly to appeal to buyers in the USA, but it was clear that there was demand for cars with the luxury of two-pedal control in Britain as well. No proprietary automatic gearboxes were made in Britain before Borg Warner opened a factory at

The 90 lost its distinguishing foglamp for 1957. This one has the original style of two-tone paint that remained optional that year and has extra-tall mirrors that no doubt helped when towing a caravan.

The original style of two-tone paint is seen again on one of the new models, in this case a 105R.

Letchworth in 1956, and as a result several companies decided to develop their own. Rover was among them.

The prototype transmission was tested on a car known as the Torque Converter 90, but it soon became clear that acceleration was poor. The solution was to uprate the 90 engine with twin carburettors, higher-compression pistons, bigger inlet valves and a bigger-bore exhaust for good measure. In this guise, the 2.6-litre engine gave between 5 per cent and 6 per cent more power and torque than the 90 type – not a huge improvement, but enough.

On the one hand, this engine was coupled with the new Roverdrive automatic gearbox to make the 105R model (the 105 approximated to the brake horsepower figure, and the

Left: With the two new models also came a new style of bonnet side identification, which was repeated on the boot lid.

Below: The twin-carburettor engine reverted to an oil-bath air filter, perhaps to aid refinement.

R was for Roverdrive). On the other, it was used with the 90's existing four-speed manual gearbox and overdrive to make the high-performance 105S (the S probably stood for Synchromesh). Although 95 mph and a 0-60 mph time of about 15.5 seconds may not sound blisteringly quick by modern standards, they were impressive for a big luxury saloon in 1956. Both cars also gained better brakes with a Girling servo that gave faster response than the Clayton type then standard on the 90. Priced above the 90, with the De Luxe version of the 105R as the most expensive Rover on offer, they also helped to prepare the buying public for the forthcoming and even pricier P5 3-litre model that was then under development.

The various automatics that British makers developed in the mid-1950s were not as sophisticated as those from the USA, and have often been derided. The Roverdrive was at least reliable and relatively simple, but it did not allow the twin-carburettor engine to give of its best, and acceleration of a 105R was very similar to that of the four-cylinder 60. The system consisted of a torque converter, a servo-operated clutch, a two-speed and reverse synchromesh manual gearbox and a Laycock overdrive like that of the 90.

Above left: New for 1957 were Diakon plastic grille badges, seen in this case on a 1958 75.

Above right: The 105S had a grille badge in the same colour as the 60, 75 and 90...

Right: ...but the top-model 105R had its own special colours. (Adrian Mitchell)

Only the top gear of the main gearbox was normally used, but a selector lever mounted under the dashboard allowed the lower ratio (called Emergency Low) to be selected manually for such things as hill climbing and descents. The overdrive could be kicked down just as on a manual P4, to provide acceleration at higher speeds – although *Autocar* magazine complained of a 'noticeable lack of urge' when they tried this manoeuvre, and main-road overtaking required a good degree of anticipation. Writing for *The Sunday Times* of 13 October 1957, Stirling Moss highlighted the car's slow step-off from rest, which he found 'rather alarming ... it takes an agonisingly long time to get across a road intersection from standstill'. Otherwise, many road tests commented on how restful the car was to drive.

The 105R could be ordered with a De Luxe specification, which brought individual front seats instead of the standard bench, a cigarette lighter, twin foglamps and Ace wheel trim rings. All these items were standard on the 105S. The two new models also pioneered a new grille badge, made from painted Perspex instead of enamelled metal and known as the Diakon type. For the 105R, there was a special departure, too, as the badge had a brown background instead of the standard black one, and the Viking ship had a yellow sail instead of a red one. Diakon grille badges would gradually appear on the other models, starting with the 90 in spring 1957 and following for the 60 and 75 during the 1958 season.

One further change took place part-way through the 1957 season, and it was an important one. The seat upholstery was completely changed, taking on pleated centre panels with horseshoe-shaped plain surround sections. The exact date of the changeover is not clear, but the new seats were certainly present on road test cars in February 1957, and it is likely that they were first used on production in January or perhaps immediately after the Christmas break. The changeover may have been made gradually, with the new style arriving first on the more expensive models, while old stock was used up on those further down the range.

PERFORMANCE FIGURES – 105S AND 105R

Road tests of the two top-model P4s in 1957 failed to match the performance claims that Rover made for the cars. The table below provides a comparison; the figures under 'Rover' were the ones provided to salesmen in a May 1957 booklet; the 105S road test in *The Motor* was dated 13 February 1957 and the 105R test was in the 24 July 1957 issue.

	105S		105R	
	Rover	*Motor*	Rover	*Motor*
0–50 mph	11.5 sec	11.9 sec	17.1 sec	17.4 sec
0–60 mph	15.0 secs	15.4 sec	23.0 sec	23.1 sec
Max speed	100 mph	95.7 mph	Not quoted	93.7 mph
Fuel cons	18–25 mpg	23.7 mpg	18–24 mpg	20.1 mpg

The 1958 Models

Sales of the P4 range for 1957 inevitably suffered from concerns about petrol availability in the wake of the Suez Crisis, and it may be that the 105R suffered disproportionately because its fuel consumption was relatively poor. Nevertheless, it was still heading the five-model range for 1958, which was now made up of the 60, 75, 90, 105S and 105R. The 1958 models also brought a wider range of the two-tone colour schemes that were becoming popular, and these were accompanied by a new colour split.

Ever since the introduction of the first two-tone models in late 1952, the roof had carried the contrast colour. Now, a slim chrome-on-brass moulding highlighted a natural dividing line running across the tops of the wings and wing pressings and ran down the nose of each front wing. The result was some of the most elegant and attractive colour schemes ever seen on the P4 range. Cars painted in a single colour did not initially have these chrome mouldings, but from early in 1958 they became standard on all models. However, only the two-tone cars had a continuation strip below the sidelights on the nose of each front wing.

Above: This 105S proudly displays the revised two-tone colour style introduced for the 1958 models. Twin auxiliary lamps were standard on these cars, together with wheel trim rings.

Right: Exports remained healthy, and this 90 was pictured in the showroom of Annand & Thompson in Queensland, Australia. The wheel trim rings are different from those on the 105S pictured above, and leave no gap around the hubcap for the painted wheel to show through. (via Alex Massey)

Pastel shades made their appearance for 1958, and suited this 75 perfectly.

For 1958, David Bache experimented with some pastel colours that were fashionable at the time, but P4 buyers were largely unimpressed. Fawn, Pale Green, and Parchment therefore remained rare and lasted for just the one season. The 1958 models also brought a switch to a washable vinyl headlining in place of the earlier wool cloth type. It was a practical move, and all headlinings now came in the same cream colour, but there were some grumbles about cheapness and modernity from Rover traditionalists.

In the 1957 season, sales of the 105R had come second to those of the best-selling 90, but for 1958 they slipped badly. In that season, the 105R was the second slowest-selling P4 model, outselling only the 75. Clearly, the novelty of the automatic transmission had boosted sales in the model's first year, but perhaps the reality of its lacklustre performance proved a hindrance to customer take-up during 1958.

A New Companion

Rover introduced its new 3-litre model at the Earl's Court Motor Show in October 1958. Priced above the P4 range, and aimed at a slightly different sector of the market, its arrival nevertheless prompted some changes to the older Rovers.

The biggest change was at the top of the range, where both the 105S and 105R models were dropped for the 1959 season. The 3-litre's automatic gearbox option, made by Borg Warner in Britain, was a far better proposition than the Roverdrive, and so the 105R had to go. Then, to maintain a clear price differential between the P4 range and the new P5, the 105S was stripped of some of its equipment to become a plain 105, with a bench front seat as standard. In the Motor Show catalogue, a 105 was priced at £1,628 17s inclusive of Purchase Tax while the cheapest (manual) 3-litre was £1,763 17s. At the bottom of the four-model P4 range, a 1959-model 60 cost £1,349 17s.

The 1959 season would be the last one for the Rover freewheel, which by this time had become something of an anachronism in the car industry even though long-term Rover owners swore by it. Most of the 1959 P4s were ordered with overdrive, at least on the home market, and for this year the 90 shared the faster-acting Girling servo of the 105 models. For the first time, the 6.00 × 16 tyres were supplemented by an optional fatter 6.40 × 15 size.

The arrival of the 3-litre was also accompanied by some cosmetic changes that David Bache had drawn up to emphasise the family resemblance between the P4 and P5 ranges. The most obvious ones were a recessed radiator grille and redesigned bumpers with new Wilmot Breeden over-riders. At the back of the car, a chromed embellisher above the number-plate echoed the similar feature on the P5 and had the additional benefit of emphasising the horizontal and making the P4s look less tall and narrow than they really were. Then on the inside, there was another new upholstery style that was accompanied by a padded section covered in black vinyl on the top of the wooden dashboard. Theoretically, this was supposed to be crash padding, but it is doubtful whether it would have been very effective in that role!

Right: The 1959 models took on a recessed grille and new bumpers and over-riders – all features shared with the new P5 3-litre. This press photograph was issued to illustrate them.

Above left: A 1959-model 75 shows the new rear-end detail, with a chrome finisher above the number-plate. Again, this reinforced the family likeness to the 3-litre.

Above right: Also new for 1959 were these seats, with a further revised upholstery pattern. When individual front seats were fitted, as here, they came with folding armrests.

Then there were new paint colours, and the two-tone options were renamed 'duo-tones'. David Bache again tried to persuade customers that brown was a good colour for a P4, this time using two new shades, but there was not a lot of interest in his efforts. Duo-tone cars were very popular, though, and as the 1959 season progressed, the original chrome-on-brass dividing strips were replaced by less expensive stainless-steel items.

Inevitably perhaps, sales of the six-cylinder cars began to fall, as more and more Rover buyers were tempted by the new 3-litre. Export sales were also down, and overseas assembly from CKD kits totalled just thirty-six cars, all shipped to Lincoln & Nolan in Dublin. It was undeniable that the P4 was beginning to look old alongside the latest offerings from manufacturers on the European continent. Few cars in its class still had separate-chassis construction (and indeed the 3-litre used a monocoque structure), and the latest challengers were lower and sleeker looking.

Yet in Britain there was still a strong band of conservatively-minded car buyers who saw in the P4 that unique blend of upright British qualities that still endears the cars to enthusiasts today. When *The Motor* tested a 60, the entry-level model of the P4 range, it reported that this was 'a car capable of giving lasting satisfaction to fastidious motorists,' and that it offered 'a very quiet and effortless cruising speed of 60 mph (with a maximum in the upper 70s) and entirely adequate acceleration coupled with a potentially greater measure of fuel economy [than the six-cylinder P4s]'. There was clearly plenty of life in the car yet.

Interesting Sidelines

The sort of hopes that Maurice Wilks had once entertained for expansion of the P4 range were fading by this time. There were no further factory-initiated experiments with coupé or drophead coupé bodies like the ones commissioned from Tickford and Pinin Farina earlier in the decade. Yet the P4 range did serve as the basis of a pair of interesting cars that are worthy of comment.

One of these was an experimental diesel-engine model that was created and run by the Engineering Department. It started life as a 1956-model 60, but was updated visually with the later style of front wings and was given a Land Rover diesel engine. Some of those who remember it believe it was a 'mileage' car, intended purely to test an experimental engine over as many miles as possible (in which case, surely a Land Rover could have done the job just as well). Others believe its purpose was to investigate the viability of a diesel-engine P4 for taxi use, possibly in Brazil.

One way or another, no diesel P4 ever entered production, but the car passed through the hands of two Rover engineers and was then sold outside the company. Its next owner remembers that it 'was lovely to drive and for a big heavy car, economical on fuel, managing about 45 miles to the gallon.'

The other car of interest was a convertible, built by the Swiss coachbuilder Graber. One engineer who saw it at the Rover factory in about 1957 recalls it as having some similarities to the Graber body design then used by Alvis. It was subsequently sighted in 1960 in France, wearing Swiss registration plates, and then again in Britain the following year. That it was painted dark green seems clear, but no more details of it have so far come to light.

CHAPTER 6

The 80 and 100, 1960–62

Two major factors influenced the shape of the 1960 P4 range. One was that Rover expected the arrival of the new 3-litre P5 in autumn 1958 to have an impact on overall P4 sales – and events would prove them right as sales shrank by a third during the 1959 season. The other was that work on the P4's successor was expected to culminate in a start to production in 1961, which meant that the older model's days already appeared to be numbered. In practice, the launch of the P6 2000 had to be delayed by two years during 1960 for reasons beyond Rover's control, but by then the company had already committed to what was intended to be a run-out range of P4 models.

With these factors in mind, it made sense to simplify the P4 range at the same time as updating it. The 1959 range had consisted of four models, the four-cylinder 60 and the six-cylinder 75, 90 and 105. For 1960, the range would be cut back to one four-cylinder model and one six-cylinder model, but both would be updated with the new engines that were now available on the Solihull production lines.

The four-cylinder engine had entered production in 1958 for the Land Rover, and had been drawn up in the middle of the decade primarily for that vehicle. It used a modern pushrod overhead-valve layout and had been designed deliberately so that a diesel version could use the same basic architecture. The diesel engine had entered production in 2.0-litre form for Land Rovers in 1957, but by omitting its 'wet' cylinder liners the block could be enlarged to 2.25 litres. In petrol 2.25-litre form, it first appeared in the Series II Land Rovers during 1958. With 77 bhp, it offered nearly as much power as the six-cylinder engine in the 75, and a good deal more than the four-cylinder in the 60. So, barely altered from its Land Rover form but for different carburation, this engine became the choice for the 1960-season entry-level P4, which was given the name of Rover 80.

The six-cylinder engine also had an interesting history. When a 3-litre capacity was needed for the forthcoming P5 model in the mid-1950s, it became clear that the existing IOE engine could not be satisfactorily enlarged without a major redesign. So Rover committed to that redesign, drawing up a new cylinder block with repositioned bore centres and increasing the number of main bearings from four to seven to further improve the IOE engine's legendary smooth running. This engine appeared in the new Rover 3-litre in autumn 1958; work then went ahead to produce a short-stroke derivative of it that would match the 2.6-litre capacity of the existing four-bearing engine. This engine gave 104 bhp

By the time of the 80 and 100, separate-chassis construction was very definitely old hat. So Rover emphasised that the P4's chassis was 'immensely strong and rigid, and affords a very high degree of safety.' This 100 chassis shows the new dished hubcaps introduced with these models.

Above: The four-cylinder engine of the 80 was shared with the Land Rover Series II that had been introduced in 1958. This display cutaway shows the car version with its long gearbox and overdrive unit.

Left: Disc brakes at the front gave the cars a more modern appeal, although they were never as colourful as the sales brochure made out!

Not much appeared to be new under the bonnet of the 100. The radiator header tank, polished here, would have had a black finish when new.

in production form, allowing it to replace both the 93 bhp 90 and the 108 bhp 105 types in a new model called the 100.

Although the 1960 models were comfortingly familiar, and even had the same paint and interior colour options as the 1959 range, they did have a number of changes from the models that had gone before. The most obvious visual change was to the wheels, which now had dished faces and different hubcaps to suit; these were shared with the 3-litre models, and had recessed black plastic centre badges rather than the painted brass ones used since the P4's introduction in 1949. The 100 had bright metal script identification on its bonnet sides and boot lid, but the 80 had none; otherwise, it was impossible to tell the two cars apart.

Those new wheels were of course not a purely cosmetic change. They had been made necessary by a switch to disc brakes at the front. This was part of a broader policy, as the 3-litre P5 changed from an all-drum system to take front discs at the same time. The disc brakes were not compatible with the earlier Rover wheels and required a different wheel offset. That in turn would have altered the rear track on the P4 unacceptably, so the 80 and 100 both came with a new and wider rear axle. With the disc brakes also came a vacuum brake servo as standard, to overcome the higher pedal pressures that such systems typically required.

When the cars were announced in October 1959, promotional literature offered both overdrive and non-overdrive versions, but that same month Rover took the decision to make overdrive standard on both of them. A few early cars had been built with the non-overdrive specification, the 80s having the same axle ratio as the overdrive variants

The new 100, finished as so many were in two-tone paint. The bonnet side and bootlid badges followed the style established with the 105R and 105S.

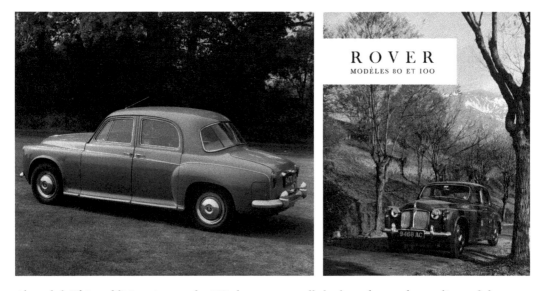

Above left: This publicity picture of a 100 shows very well the homely yet elegant lines of the later P4 models.

Above right: A single-colour 100 nevertheless graced the cover of this sales brochure, which was produced in French for export markets.

Above: This dashboard could belong to an 80 or a 100 – there were no obvious differences. The tool tray under the dashboard had long had a finisher to match the wood, and the optional radio here is a push-button set.

Right: Every P4 came with this helpful card when new, showing how to operate the heater controls.

but the 100s having the taller 3.9:1 gearing as used in the earlier 90 without overdrive. More would in fact be built later, but not for the home market; there were 101 non-overdrive 100s for Australia during the 1962 season, for example.

On the inside, everything was once again familiar P4 fare. A front bench seat was standard on both models, with individual seats an extra-cost option. Two features would, however, stand out to anyone familiar with the P4 range who tried out one of these new models. First, the separate starter button had gone and the cars were started by the ignition key – a feature introduced with the 3-litre in 1958 and one that was increasingly becoming the norm on cars generally. The second new feature was a more powerful blower fan for the heating and ventilating system, which was a very welcome change.

Changes

The 80 and the 100 were more or less 'right' from the off, as indeed they should have been because Rover had been building P4s for ten years when they were introduced. Not much was therefore changed in their three-year production run apart from colour schemes and small details of the specification. Even the prices stayed the same for the first two years.

So saying, there certainly were some changes, and many of them were made to increase commonality with the 3-litre models and so reduce manufacturing costs. The ones that deserve mention are the deletion of the reflective chrome 'pips' from the front wings, which occurred some time around Easter 1960, and the standardisation of safety-belt mountings on the 1961 models. The belts themselves (initially rather cumbersome items made by the Irvin parachute company) were available by the end of 1961 for cars with the standard bench front seat, but it would be a few more months before a set became available to suit the optional individual seats. Belts certainly were available for the rear seat as well, but were very rarely ordered.

The 80 suffered its fair share of engine modifications. The noise issue identified in early road tests was traced to the timing chain, and so modifications were made to deal with this. Then there was a problem with flat spots in acceleration and with a tendency for the carburettor to ice up, and so in early 1961 a different carburettor was fitted, and no doubt some earlier cars were also converted to use this.

During 1961, a new road wheel design was introduced (although its differences from the original were not obvious without a close look) and, somewhat bizarrely, this developed a reputation for cracking around the stud holes. A third type was not introduced until approximately 1963, distinguished by reinforcements around the stud holes, and no doubt many of the original wheels on surviving cars were replaced in service.

Two other changes deserve comment, and both were made at the start of the 1962 season. The one that causes considerable confusion is the 'Mark IV model' identification on the chassis number plates of 80s and 100s from this year. Exactly why the Mark IV name was introduced is not clear even now, but what is clear is that the Mark IV models had a number of electrical differences from earlier 80s and 100s.

The second change was to the chassis numbering system. All earlier P4s had been given chassis numbers with a four-figure prefix code, and the fourth figure of that code revealed the season in which the car had been built. So a 6450 prefix was for a 1960-model 80 and a 6451 prefix was for a 1961 model. As it was now becoming Rover practice to introduce

 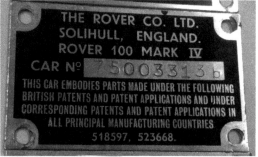

Above left: The chassis number plate of a 1960-model 100 shows the original numbering system... (Alan Milstead)

Above right: ...while this one, from a 1962 car, shows the new numbering system with a suffix letter, and also that the 1962 cars were known as Mk IV types. Note also that the company's location is now shown as Solihull rather than Birmingham, although the factory was still the same one. (Alan Milstead)

running changes on production and not to wait until the model-year changeover, the 1962 and later cars had a three-figure prefix code that identified the type (745 for an 80) and there was no year identifier. Instead, production changes that were of importance for the maintenance of the car were identified by a suffix letter code. On the 1962-season 80 and 100, the serial numbers were all initially followed by an A suffix (in practice a lower-case 'a') and changed to a B suffix when different disc brake callipers were fitted in March 1962.

PERFORMANCE FIGURES – 80 AND 100

Road tests of the 80 and 100 did not always bear out the performance claims that Rover made in their booklets for salesmen; the 80, for example, turned out to have a higher top speed than predicted, while the 100 did not quite reach the Rover estimate. The table below provides a comparison; in all cases, the figures are for cars with overdrive.

	80		100	
	Rover	*Autocar*	Rover	*Motor*
0–50 mph	16.5 sec	17.4 sec	12.5 sec	12.1 sec
0–60 mph	25.0 secs	22.8 sec	17.0 sec	17.6 sec
Max speed	82 mph	85.8 mph	94 mph	92.1 mph
Fuel cons	18–25 mpg	18–26 mpg	18–25 mpg	20.6 mpg

A Qualified Success

In the eyes of motoring journalists, age was now counting against the P4. *The Motor* referred to the 'traditional appearance and amenities' of the 100 it tested, though admitted they were 'blended with up-to-date mechanical features.' Even Bill Boddy of *Motor Sport*, a staunch supporter of the P4, noted that 'its appearance has dated', and his October 1961 review of a 100 added that 'my first impression ... was that the manufacturers must be optimistic to go on listing such an old-fashioned car'. Yet he went on to enjoy the car very much and concluded that, 'if you can see real merit in the more spacious old-fashioned car but are afraid of vintage idiosyncrasies, and also want decent braking and performance, this is the car for you.'

Opinions of the 80 were mixed. Some reviewers found the engine noisy or rough – neither of which should be the case with one that has been properly maintained and set up. It was not as smooth as the six-cylinder cars, but no four-cylinder engine of that period ever was as smooth as a six, and in some ways the car was more enjoyable to drive than the 100 because the lighter-engined car was less inclined to understeer and was rather less tiring to manoeuvre at parking speeds.

With the benefit of hindsight, though, the 100 was a superb machine, and today many P4 aficionados claim that it was the best all-rounder of the entire range. It had most of the performance of the earlier twin-carburettor 105S, 'and will accomplish it with less effort' as

The P4 was so well established that there was no need for a picture of the car on this 1962 sales brochure – a drawing of the steering wheel was enough.

The Autocar put it. The servo-assisted brakes with discs at the front gave excellent stopping power, and the petrol consumption was likely to be lower than that of the admittedly faster 110 that replaced it in autumn 1962.

The buying public seemed to agree on the relative merits of the two models. In the three years of 100 production, 16,621 examples of the car found buyers; but by contrast, just 5,888 examples of the 80 were built in the same period. By the time Rover came to plan their successors, it was abundantly clear that what the buyers wanted was smooth six-cylinders, and so the 80 would be the last of the four-cylinder P4s when it went out of production in mid-1962.

There was very little demand for the P4 overseas by the time the 80 and 100 entered production, because so many more modern cars were available in the 2.0-litre to 2.5-litre engine capacity bracket. Just 524 export-model 80s and 2,631 of their 100 counterparts were made in the three years of production. Among these, the only overseas assembly was in Ireland, where the Standard Motor Company of Dublin had taken over from Lincoln & Nolan and built just fifteen 80s (all 1960 models) and eighty-one 100s.

Once it had become clear that the new Rover 2000 was not going to be introduced at the planned date of October 1961 but would be delayed until October 1963, Rover's strategy for the P4 range changed. Instead of fading out in 1962 after a year of overlap with the new model, it would now have to have its life extended into 1964. So work began on developments that would prolong the appeal of the cars so that Rover did not lose its position in the market.

Jim Shaw was still the Project Engineer in charge of the P4 range, and it was his job to propose changes that would deal with the aspects of the current P4s that were causing customer dissatisfaction. One of those causes of dissatisfaction was heavy steering – Bill Boddy had commented in *Motor Sport* that the 100's steering was 'fearfully heavy for parking', although there were few complaints of that sort about the 80 because it had less engine weight over the front wheels. It seems likely that there had been a change in customer expectations, because these were not the sort of complaints that had been particularly common about earlier P4s, and in fact similar complaints were coming in about the steering on the 3-litre P5, too.

Rover's first reaction was to lower the steering box ratio in the late spring of 1960, a change made on both the 80 and 100 in the interests of common componentry. The next stage was to investigate fitting them both with the same power-assisted steering that was being developed for the P5 cars. This was actually signed off as part of the specification for the 1962 models but never entered production. Most likely is that it was cancelled because of increased costs, because of differentiation from the more expensive 3-litre, and because there was no power-assisted steering in the planned specification of the Rover 2000 that would replace it a year later.

One other option was explored in late 1960, and that was the availability of an automatic gearbox for the 100; no consideration seems to have been given to offering it in the 80, probably because the four-cylinder engine did not deliver enough of the torque that was so important for an automatic gearbox to work effectively. It seems likely that Rover's choice would have fallen on the new Borg Warner Type 35 gearbox that became available in Britain during 1960 (the older DG type was already available as an option in the 3-litre), but one way or the other, the idea withered on the vine.

CHAPTER 7

A Lauded Farewell: 95 and 110 Models, 1962–64

The delayed introduction of the new Rover 2000 meant that Rover had to extend the life of the P4 range, and they did so with two new models that were introduced at the September 1962 Earl's Court Motor Show. This had a to be a minimum-cost exercise, but on the other hand it also had to deliver some convincing new models that would maintain Rover's position in the market for cars with a pre-tax cost of between £1,000 and £1,200 (in Britain, these figures were of course inflated by the addition of Purchase Tax).

In these circumstances, it was not surprising that the new P4 models drew quite heavily on developments originally initiated for the Rover 3-litre, or that they continued to reflect these developments in changes that were made during their two-year production life. Their introduction preceded that of the Rover 2000 by a year, and they were sold alongside it for a further year so that Rover still had a more traditional car to offer those who found the 2000 too modern (and it was indeed a remarkably advanced design for its day).

These new models were called the Rover 95 and Rover 110, and those new numbers reflected – this time very approximately – the brake horsepower of their engines. In practice, the 95 had 102 bhp, but it could be neither a 100 nor a 105 because those two model-names had already been used; the number 95 was available and fitted the bill perfectly because the new car had a deliberately lower specification than the old 100. The 110 had all of 123 bhp, but there were several possible reasons why the numbers 120 and 125 were rejected. Not the least of them were that there had been a Jaguar XK120 within recent memory, and that these higher numbers might have led buyers to expect more performance than the production car could actually deliver.

Both the 95 and the 110 had engines derived from the 2.6-litre seven-bearing six-cylinder in the 100 that was in production while they were being developed. This engine's origin in the programme to develop the 3-litre power unit has already been mentioned, and to improve its performance Rover reused some of the changes originally intended to give the flagship model better performance.

As early as 1960, it had become clear that more power could be found in the 3-litre engine by improving its breathing. The original design used a single casting for the cylinder head and inlet manifold to save manufacturing costs, but this tended to restrict the gas flow. Rover themselves came up with a new design where the manifold was cast

Above left: Exports were at a low ebb by this time, but this magnificent 110 in Light Navy was chosen by a customer in New Zealand. The auxiliary driving lights were optional extras. Note the full-width wheel trims; they were shared with the 3-litre, and the 110 was the only P4 to have them when new.

Above right: Rear view of a 1964 110, this time in Pine Green. Two-tone options were still available, but the trend was now towards single colours.

separately from the head and bolted to it; this enabled the inner faces of the manifold to be cleaned up to improve the gas flow. To make doubly sure, Chief Engineer Maurice Wilks called in performance development expert Harry Weslake, who suggested some refinements. Weslake, whose consultancy business was based at Rye in East Sussex, was a big name in the motoring world at the time, and it made good publicity to use his name in association with the new cylinder head. So the Rover engines with which he had helped were trumpeted as 'Weslake-head' types – much to the quiet annoyance of the Rover engineers who believed they had done most of the design work!

It was a simple matter to use the Weslake head on the smaller-capacity P4 engine as well, and the result was an engine that reached its peak power at 5000 rpm rather than the 4750 rpm of the 100 type. Its larger HD8 carburettor and trumpet-type paper-element air filter both came straight from the revised 3-litre engine, and a new distributor and revised camshaft profile were added into the mix. There were some minor changes to the valves and the engineers specified a bigger-bore exhaust system. With its maximum torque developed in the middle of the rev range rather than at the bottom end, the new 110 engine was also well suited to the higher cruising speeds required of cars in the new age of the motorway in Britain.

The old 100 engine also went through a series of revisions for its new job in the 95 and, though similar, the two engines were not the same. It was given new pistons and the reprofiled camshaft developed for the 110, and although Rover claimed it was very slightly less powerful than the 100 and delivered very slightly less torque, the differences were really academic.

Both new models retained the old four-speed gearbox, though now with the bigger layshaft bearings used in the 3-litre versions. The 110 came with overdrive as standard; the 95 did not have it and could not have it as an option. Instead, it had the taller gearing of the non-overdrive 100. The new-found performance of the 110 made it prudent to delete

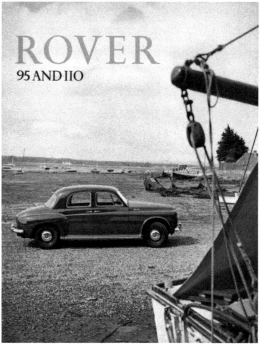

Above left: The 110 engine was the only P4 to have the Weslake-head engine, which had a distinctive twin-trumpet air cleaner box.

Above right: The cover of this sales brochure suggests relaxation and tranquillity – both qualities that buyers would readily have associated with the P4 range at the time.

Not much had changed under the bonnet of the 95, where the view closely resembled that of the 100's engine bay. (Richard Bryant)

the kickdown facility of the overdrive that had been a feature since its introduction on the 1956-model 90; otherwise, it would have been possible to over-rev the engine by kicking down at high speeds. Both cars took on a new fuel system with the twin pumps of the 3-litre that gave a respectable reserve capacity, and although both had servo-assisted brakes they managed without the vacuum reservoir fitted to earlier P4s with such a system.

Elsewhere, there was a mixture of the familiar and the (subtly) new. The popular two-tone paint combinations still cost extra, and so did individual front seats in place of the standard bench type. Although the seats looked the same as before, they actually had more padding to improve occupant location, and a new additional option was fully-reclining front seats like those available in the 3-litre. Then there were changes to the instrument panel, where the main dials were again borrowed from the 3-litre and there were some other minor alterations. Most obvious was the integration of the amber handbrake warning light into the main instrument panel, while the lights switch now incorporated a parking lights position (side and tail lights on the road side of the car) and on the 110 the washer and wiper controls were combined in a single switch. A further benefit borrowed from the 3-litre was a voltage stabiliser that prevented the wavering of the needles on the smaller gauges.

The list of changes continued. While the 95 retained the wheels, hubcaps and 6.00 × 15 tyres of the 100, the 110 came with wider 6.40 × 15 tyres as standard, as well as full-width wheel trims in stainless steel that were associated with the latest 3-litres. As these masked most of the wheel disc, 110s always had black-painted wheels rather than the body-coloured ones traditional to the P4; it reduced both cost and complication on the assembly lines. There was further cost-saving in that both 95 and 110 had the same grille badge as the 3-litre, which of course did not include a model number. New sealed-beam headlights were made standard, and a major new option was a rear-window demister (now known universally as a heated rear window) that was embedded in the glass of the central back window panel. At long last, the key number was now no longer stamped into the face of each lock, so improving theft resistance to some degree.

Press Comment

It was a lot of effort to put into a pair of cars that did not look very different from the ones they replaced. No amount of effort could of course have overcome the plain fact that the P4 was now looking rather dated – as *The Motor* pointed out in its January 1963 road test of a 110. More recent, and less expensive, big saloons from BMC had a far more modern

Bonnet side badges were in the same style for both models, but the grille badges had no model identification.

Black and discreetly British! Although the P4 was an outdated design by the time this 95 was built, it retained a distinguished air.

and sleek appearance, even if they did not enjoy the Rovers' reputation for reliability and durability. Press commentators highlighted the old-fashioned rear-hinged rear doors, which were now becoming known as 'suicide doors' because they could fly open at speed if the lock was released (typically by a curious child). Rover had designed them to give better access to the rear seats than doors hinged on the centre pillar and had protected them with childproof locks, but the bad reputation had been earned by cars of other makes.

Even so, the 95 and 110 earned their share of praise in the motoring press. *Practical Motorist* noted that their test 95 was capable of 'a burst of acceleration which belies the car's sedate appearance', and *The Motor* described the 110 as a 'surprisingly fast saloon'. Sadly, a question mark over the 110 was briefly raised when the consumer magazine *Which?* reported in its April 1963 issue that their test example had suffered from engine failure – burned piston crowns that necessitated a replacement engine. Rover investigated, and discovered that the service carried out by *Which?* had left the car with the incorrect grade of spark plugs, and these had caused the problem. *Which?* dutifully published a retraction and an apology in its June issue, but no doubt the original report had already deterred a few potential 110 customers.

Production Changes

Even though the 95 and 110 were always projected to remain in production for no more than two years, a number of specification changes – some quite major – were made during that period. Yet their original designation as 'Mk I models' remained throughout production on the chassis number plate and in the owner's handbook. That in itself raises an unanswerable question: normally, manufacturers do not call any product a 'Mk I' until it has been replaced by a Mk II!

The best known of the production changes is the introduction of steel for the bonnet, boot and door panels that occurred in approximately December 1962. Early 95s and 110s

Right: Both the 95 and 110 were Mark I models according to their chassis number plates. There never would be a Mark II. (Alan Milstead)

Below: This picture of a late 110 is a sad reminder that one effect of the change to steel panels on the final cars was a greater vulnerability to rust. This could never have happened to the aluminium alloy doors and bonnet on the earlier P4s.

had the same lightweight aluminium alloy panels as their predecessors, and the steel panels added a considerable amount of extra weight – around 165 lb of it – to cars that were already heavy. No figures are available to illustrate the damage that extra weight did to performance and petrol consumption, but there must have been some.

The change inevitably prompts the question of why it was made. P4 Project Engineer Jim Shaw remembered that there was a problem with owners denting the door panels – which can only have been caused by a change in owner behaviour because the doors had served perfectly well with aluminium alloy skins since 1949! Most likely is that recent improvements in door seals introduced by other manufacturers had led car users in general to expect to have to slam doors with some force, and that the P4 was suffering as a result. Why change the bonnet and boot as well? Perhaps because steel was cheaper than aluminium alloy and these were, after all, the run-out models...

The remaining major changes all occurred between February and April 1964, which was three months or so before the end of production. For the most part, they reflected changes elsewhere in Rover product ranges, and simply brought the P4 into line to reduce manufacturing complications. First came a change to the engines (accompanied by a change to a 'b' suffix in the P4's engine numbers), as larger main bearing journals were specified. The material specification of the differential was changed to make it 35 per cent stronger in March, and then in April the brake servo changed to the latest Girling MkIIA type, as used in the 3-litre. The only change unique to the P4 was made in March, when nylon inserts were added to the leaf springs to improve the ride: many manufacturers would simply not have bothered this late in the day, but Rover clearly wanted the cars to be as right as possible as they ended production.

The Numbers Game

Sales of the P4 range had peaked in 1960, and had been dropping steadily ever since. Nobody could have expected the 95 and 110 to halt the decline, and indeed they did not. Their first season of 1963 saw only a small reduction from the 1962 figures, but for 1964 – when they were in competition with their Rover 2000 stablemate – they fell to less than half the 1962 figure.

The final P4 was a 90, and was pictured here at the end-of-line ceremony on 27 May 1964. The assembly lines were rapidly turned over to Land Rover production.

Export sales were already vanishingly small, and Rover needed to build no more than 113 P4s with left-hand drive and 542 with right-hand drive to meet demand over the two years of 95 and 110 production. The overseas assembly operations had now ceased. So it was that the very last P4 was built on 27 May 1964 at the company's Solihull factory. It was a 95, fittingly painted in the same Charcoal Grey that had been used on the 95 that had introduced the model at Earl's Court in 1962. There was a small ceremony on the production lines, but the car itself was despatched out to a Rover dealer in the usual way and has since vanished.

PERFORMANCE FIGURES – 95 AND 110

The performance and fuel consumption figures that Rover claimed in their salesmen's booklets were slightly optimistic, but were quite close to the figures obtained in independent road tests. The table below provides a comparison; the 95 was tested in *Practical Motorist* of March 1963, and the 110 in *The Motor* of 30 January 1963.

	95		110	
	Rover	*Prac Mt'ist*	Rover	*Motor*
0–50 mph	12.9 sec	12.8 sec	11.3 sec	11.6 sec
0–60 mph	18.0 secs	18.4 sec	15.5 sec	15.9 sec
Max speed	94 mph	93 mph	105.8 mph	100 mph
Fuel cons	18–25 mpg	18–22.5 mpg	18–25 mpg	18.4–22.8 mpg

Appendix A

Technical Specifications

Engine

All engines had a cast-iron block and an aluminium alloy head.

60

1,997 cc (77.8 mm × 105 mm) four-cylinder with three main bearings, inlet over exhaust valve configuration, and single SU H4 carburettor

1954–56	6.73:1 CR, 60 bhp at 4,000 rpm, 101 lb ft at 2,000 rpm
1957–58	7.2:1 CR, 60 bhp at 4,000 rpm, 101 lb ft at 2,000 rpm
1959	6.92:1 CR, 60 bhp at 4,000 rpm, 101 lb ft at 2,000 rpm

75 (1950–54)

2,103 cc (65.2 mm × 105 mm) six-cylinder with four main bearings, inlet over exhaust valve configuration, and two SU H4 carburettors

1950–54	7.25:1 CR, 75 bhp at 4,200 rpm, 111 lb ft at 2,500 rpm

75 (1955–59)

2,230 cc (73.025 mm × 88.9 mm) six-cylinder with four main bearings, inlet over exhaust valve configuration, and single SU H6 carburettor

1955–58	6.95:1 CR, 80 bhp at 4,500 rpm, 113 lb ft at 1,750 rpm
1959	7.2:1 CR, 80 bhp at 4,500 rpm, 113 lb ft at 1,750 rpm

80

2,286 cc (90.47 mm × 88.9 mm) four-cylinder with three main bearings, overhead valve configuration, and single Solex carburettor (type PAIO-5, then PAIO-6 from March 1961)

1960–1962	77bhp at 4,250 rpm, 124 lb ft at 2,500 rpm

90

2,638 cc (73.025 mm × 105 mm) six-cylinder with four main bearings, inlet over exhaust valve configuration, and single SU H6 carburettor

1954	6.25:1 CR, 90 bhp at 4,500 rpm, 130 lb ft at 1,500 rpm
1955	6.73:1 CR, 90 bhp at 4,500 rpm, 130 lb ft at 1,500 rpm
1956–59	7.5:1 CR, 93 bhp at 4,500 rpm, 138 lb ft at 1,750 rpm

95

2,625 cc (77.8 mm × 97.025 mm) six-cylinder with seven main bearings, inlet over exhaust valve configuration, and single SU HD6 carburettor

1963–64	8.8:1 CR, 102 bhp at 4,750 rpm, 140 lb ft at 1,500 rpm
	7.8:1 CR (export option), 100 bhp, 136 lb ft

100

2,625 cc (77.8 mm × 97.025 mm) six-cylinder with seven main bearings, inlet over exhaust valve configuration, and single SU HD6 carburettor

1960–62	8.8:1 CR, 104 bhp at 4,750 rpm, 138 lb ft at 1,500 rpm
	7.8:1 CR (export option)

105R, 105S and 105

2,638 cc (73.025 mm × 105 mm) six-cylinder with four main bearings, inlet over exhaust valve configuration, and two SU HD6 carburettors

1957–59	8.5:1 CR, 108 bhp at 4,250 rpm, 152 lb ft at 2,500 rpm
	7.5:1 CR (export option)

110

2,625 cc (77.8 mm × 97.025 mm) six-cylinder with seven main bearings, inlet over exhaust valve configuration, Weslake cylinder head and single SU HD8 carburettor

1960–62	8.8:1 CR, 123 bhp at 5,000 rpm, 142 lb ft at 3,000 rpm
	7.8:1 CR (export option), 121 bhp, 136 lb ft

Gearbox

Four-speed manual (all models except 105R)
Ratios 3.37:1, 2.04:1, 1.37:1, 1.00:1, reverse 2.97:1; synchromesh on third
      and top only (1950–53), or on second, third and top (1954 on)

Freewheel standard on 75 (1950-1958), 60 (1954–58) and 90 (1954–55);
      alternative to overdrive on 1956–58 90

Overdrive (with 0.77:1 gearing) optional on 90 (1956–58) and 60 and 75
(1957–59); standard on 90 (1959), 105S and 105; standard on all 80
and 100 (except for a few early cars) and on 110.

Roverdrive three-speed automatic (105R)
    Ratios 1.74:1, 1.00:1, 0.77:1, reverse 2.90:1

Final Drive

4.3:1   60 and 75 except with overdrive; 90 except with 3.9:1 option; 105S, 105, 80, 100 and 110
3.9:1   optional on 90 from March 1954; standard on non-overdrive 100 and all
         95
4.7:1   60 and 75 with overdrive; 105R

Suspension

Independent front suspension with wishbones, coil springs and anti-roll bar
Live rear axle with constant-rate semi-elliptic leaf springs and (1950–53 only) Panhard
    rod

Steering

Burman recirculating-ball, worm and nut steering with variable ratio

Brakes

11-in drum brakes on all four wheels (1950–59)
10.7-in disc front brakes and 11-in drum rear brakes (1960–64)
Hydraulically operated front brakes and mechanically operated rear brakes (1950
    models)
All-hydraulic system (1951 and later models)
Vacuum servo standard with overdrive from 1956, and on 105R

Wheels and Tyres

Five-stud disc wheels with 15-in diameter and 4.5-in rim
6.00 × 15 crossply tyres standard; 6.40 × 15 size optional from 1959 and standard on 110

Dimensions

Overall length	178.25 in (4,527 mm), 1950–59
	178.625 in (4,537 mm), 1960–64
Overall width	65.325 in (1,659 mm)
Overall height	63.25 in (1,606 mm)
Wheelbase	111 in (2,819 mm)
Front track	52 in (1,321 mm) with drum brakes
	52.5 in (1,333 mm) with disc brakes
Rear track	51.5 in (1,308 mm)

Weight

60

1954	3,062 lb (1389 kg)
1955–56	3,073 lb (1394 kg)
1957–58	3,106 lb (1409 kg)
1957–58 with overdrive	3,148 lb (1428 kg)
1959	3,062 lb (1389 kg)
1959 with overdrive	3,104 lb (1408 kg)

75

1950–51	3,108 lb (1,410 kg)
1952–54	3,200 lb (1,451 kg)
1955–56	3,229 lb (1,465 kg)
1957–58	3,262 lb (1,480 kg)
1957–58 with overdrive	3,304 lb (1,499 kg)
1959	3,216 lb (1,459 kg)
1959 with overdrive	3,258 lb (1,478 kg)

80

1960–62	3,204 lb (1,453kg)
1960–62 with overdrive	3,246 lb (1,472kg)

90

1954–55	3,200 lb (1,451 kg)
1956 with overdrive	3,276 lb (1,486 kg)
1957–58	3,267 lb (1,482 kg)
1957–58 with overdrive	3,309 lb (1,501 kg)
1959	3,237 lb (1,468 kg)
1959 with overdrive	3,279 lb (1,487 kg)

95

1963–1964	3,287 lb (1,490 kg)

100

1960–62	3,267 lb (1,482 kg)
1960–62 with overdrive	3,309 lb (1,501 kg)

105R, 105S and 105

1957–58 105R	3,420 lb (1,551 kg)
1957–58 105R De Luxe	3,473 lb (1,575 kg)
1957–58 105S	3,382 lb (1,533 kg)
1959 105	3,284 lb (1,490 kg)

110

1963–64	3,354 lb (1,521 kg)

APPENDIX B

Identification

All P4 chassis numbers had a prefix code that identified the model and sub-type. The chassis number will be found on the plate attached to the passenger's side A-pillar (hinge pillar for the front door). Dates shown here are for the Rover 'season', usually now called the model-year, which ran from September to the following August.

1950

Four-digit serial numbers, prefixed by:

0430	75	0530	2.6-litre prototype

Export models had an L (LHD) or R (RHD) prefix, e.g. L04300016.

1951

Four-digit serial numbers, prefixed by:

1430	75 Home Market	1436	75 RHD Export
1433	75 LHD Export	1466	75 RHD CKD

1952

Four-digit serial numbers, prefixed by:

2430	75 Home Market	2463	75 LHD CKD
2433	75 LHD Export	2466	75 RHD CKD
2436	75 RHD Export		

1953

Four-digit serial numbers, prefixed by:

3430	75 Home Market	3463	75 LHD CKD
3433	75 LHD Export	3466	75 RHD CKD
3436	75 RHD Export		

1954

Four-digit serial numbers, prefixed by:

4330	60 Home Market	4336	60 RHD Export
4333	60 LHD Export	4366	60 RHD CKD
4430	75 Home Market	4436	75 RHD Export
4433	75 LHD Export	4476	75 RHD CKD
4530	90 Home Market	4536	90 RHD Export
4533	90 LHD Export	4586	90 RHD CKD

1955

Four-digit serial numbers, prefixed by:

5330	60 Home Market	5336	60 RHD Export
5333	60 LHD Export	5366	60 RHD CKD
5430	75 Home Market	5436	75 RHD Export
5433	75 LHD Export	5476	75 RHD CKD
5530	90 Home Market	5536	90 RHD Export
5533	90 LHD Export	5586	90 RHD CKD

1956

Four-digit serial numbers, prefixed by:

3306	60 Home Market	3366	60 RHD Export
3336	60 LHD Export	3376	60 RHD CKD
3406	75 Home Market	3466	75 RHD Export
3436	75 LHD Export	3476	75 RHD CKD
6530	90 Home Market	3566	90 RHD Export
3506	90 Home Market	3576	90 RHD CKD
3536	90 LHD Export		

(The 6530 prefix was used for only sixteen cars.)

1957

Four-digit serial numbers, prefixed by:

6007	60 Home Market	6027	60 RHD CKD
6017	60 RHD Export	6037	60 LHD Export

6057	75 Home Market	6077	75 RHD CKD
6067	75 RHD Export	6087	75 LHD Export
6107	90 Home Market	6127	90 RHD CKD
6117	90 RHD Export	6137	90 LHD Export
6157	105R Home Market	6187	105R LHD Export
6167	105R RHD Export		
6207	105S Home Market	6237	105S LHD Export
6217	105S RHD Export		

1958

Four-digit serial numbers, prefixed by:

6008	60 Home Market	6038	60 LHD Export
6018	60 RHD Export		
6058	75 Home Market	6088	75 LHD Export
6068	75 RHD Export		
6108	90 Home Market	6128	90 RHD CKD
6118	90 RHD Export	6138	90 LHD Export
6158	105R Home Market	6188	105R LHD Export
6168	105R RHD Export		
6208	105S Home Market	6238	105S LHD Export
6218	105S RHD Export		

1959

Four-digit serial numbers, prefixed by:

6009	60 Home Market	6029	60 RHD CKD
6019	60 RHD Export	6039	60 LHD Export
6059	75 Home Market	6089	75 LHD Export
6069	75 RHD Export		
6109	90 Home Market	6129	90 RHD CKD
6119	90 RHD Export	6139	90 LHD Export
6209	105 Home Market	6229	105 RHD CKD
6219	105 RHD Export	6239	105 LHD Export

1960

Four-digit serial numbers, prefixed by:

6450	80 Home Market	6470	80 RHD CKD
6460	80 RHD Export	6480	80 LHD Export
6500	100 Home Market	6520	100 RHD CKD
6510	100 RHD Export	6530	100 LHD Export

1961

Four-digit serial numbers, prefixed by:

6451	80 Home Market	6481	80 LHD Export
6461	80 RHD Export		
6501	100 Home Market	6521	100 RHD CKD
6511	100 RHD Export	6531	100 LHD Export

1962

Five-digit serial numbers, with prefixes as below and letter suffix 'a' (to March 1962) or 'b' (from March 1962).

745	80 Home Market	748	80 LHD Export
746	80 RHD Export		
750	100 Home Market	752	100 RHD CKD
751	100 RHD Export	753	100 LHD Export

1963–1964

Five-digit serial numbers, with prefixes as below and letter suffix 'a' (to March 1964) or 'b' (from March 1964).

760	95 Home Market	763	95 LHD Export
761	95 RHD Export		
765	110 Home Market	768	110 LHD Export
766	110 RHD Export		

Appendix C

Paint and Trim Colours

1950 Season

Paint	Trim
Black	Green, Grey or Red
Connaught Green	Grey
Ivory	Green or Red
Lakeside Green	Green
Pastel Blue	Blue

1951 Season

Paint	Trim
Black	Beige, Blue, Green, Grey or Red
Connaught Green	Green or Grey
Ivory	Green or Red
Lakeside Green	Green
Pastel Blue	Blue

1952 Season

Paint	Trim
Black	Blue, Green, Grey, Red or Tan
Connaught Green	Green or Grey
Ivory	Green or Red
Lakeside Green	Green
Pastel Blue	Blue

1953 Season

Paint	*Trim*
Black	Blue, Green, Grey, Red or Tan
Ivory	Green, Red or Tan
Light Grey	Blue, Green, Grey or Red
Pastel Blue	Blue
Sage Green	Green, Grey, Red or Tan

Two-tones	
Dark Grey over Light Grey	Blue, Green, Grey or Red
Sage Green over Light Green	Green, Grey, Red or Tan

1954 Season

Paint	*Trim*
Black	Blue, Green, Grey, Red or Tan
Grey	Grey
Ivory	Green, Red or Tan
Pastel Blue	Blue
Sage Green	Green

Two-tones	
Dark Grey over Grey	Grey
Sage Green over Light Green	Green

1955 Season

Paint	*Trim*
Black	Blue, Green, Grey, Red or Tan
Grey	Grey
Ivory	Green, Red or Tan
Sage Green	Green
Smoke Blue	Blue

Two-tones	
Dark Grey over Grey	Grey
Sage Green over Light Green	Green

1956 Season, 1957 Season and 1958 Season to March 1958

Sales literature did not specify the interior colour options with each exterior colour, but listed the interior colours as Blue, Green, Grey, Red and Tan. Some combinations were probably not available on the grounds of good taste.

Single-tone

Black	Ivory
Dark Grey	Sage Green
Dove Grey	Smoke Blue
French Grey	

Two-tone

Grey over Grey   Grey interior
(It is not clear which two Greys were used for the exterior.)

1958 Season from April 1958

Sales literature did not specify the interior colour options with each exterior colour, but listed the interior colours as Blue, Green, Grey, Red and Tan. Some combinations were probably not available on the grounds of good taste.

Single-tone

Black	Pale Green
Blue	Parchment
Dove Grey	Sage Green
Fawn	Smoke Grey

Two-tones

Dove Grey over Smoke Grey	Pale Green over Sage Green
Fawn over Black	Smoke Grey over Black
Fawn over Parchment	

1959 Season and 1960 Season

Sales literature did not specify the interior colour options with each exterior colour, but listed the interior colours as Beige, Mid-Blue, Red, Rush Green and Silver Grey. Some combinations were probably not available on the grounds of good taste.

Single-tone

Black	Light Brown
Dark Blue	Light Grey
Dove Grey	Rush Green
Dover White	Shadow Green
Heather Brown	Smoke Grey

Duo-tones

Dark Blue over Black	Light Grey over Dove Grey
Dark Blue over Light Grey	Light Grey over Dover White
Dover Grey over Smoke Grey	Rush Green over Black

Heather Brown over Light Brown   Rush Green over Shadow Green
Light Brown over Black   Smoke Grey over Black
Light Grey over Dark Brown

1961 Season and 1962 Season to February 1962

Sales literature did not specify the interior colour options with each exterior colour, but listed the interior colours as Blue, Green, Grey, Red and Tan. Some combinations were probably not available on the grounds of good taste.

Single-tone

Black	Rush Green
Ivory	Shadow Green
Medium Grey	Slate Grey
Norse Blue	Smoke Grey
Royal Blue	Storm Grey

Duo-tones

Ivory over Medium Grey	Slate Grey over Royal Blue
Medium Grey over Storm Grey	Slate Grey over Storm Grey
Rush Green over Shadow Green	Smoke Grey over Black

1962 Season from March 1962

Paint	*Trim*
Black	Blue, Green, Grey, Red or Tan
Burgundy	Grey or Red
Ivory	Blue, Green, Red or Tan
Light Navy	Blue, Grey or Tan
Medium Grey	Blue, Green, Grey, Red or Tan
Pine Green	Green, Grey or Tan
Shadow Green	Green, Grey or Tan
Slate Grey	Blue, Grey or Red
Smoke Grey	Blue, Green, Grey, Red or Tan
Storm Grey	Blue, Green, Grey, Red or Tan

Duo-tones

Ivory over Medium Grey	Blue, Green, Red or Tan
Ivory over Storm Grey	Blue, Green, Red or Tan
Medium Grey over Burgundy	Grey or Red
Medium Grey over Light Navy	Blue, Grey or Tan
Medium Grey over Pine Green	Green, Grey or Tan
Medium Grey over Storm Grey	Blue, Green, Grey, Red or Tan

Shadow Green over Pine Green	Green, Grey or Tan
Slate Grey over Light Navy	Blue, Grey or Tan
Slate Grey over Storm Grey	Blue, Grey or Red
Smoke Grey over Black	Blue, Green, Grey, Red or Tan

1963 Season and 1964 Season

Paint	*Trim*
Black	Blue, Green, Red, Stone or Tan
Burgundy	Grey, Red or Stone
Charcoal	Blue, Green, Grey, Red or Stone
Juniper Green	Green, Grey, Stone or Tan
Light Navy	Blue, Grey or Stone
Marine Grey	Blue, Green, Grey, Red, Stone or Tan
Pine Green	Green, Grey, Stone or Tan
Stone Grey	Blue, Green, Red or Tan
Steel Blue	Blue, Grey, Red or Tan
White	Blue, Green, Red, Stone or Tan

Duo-tones	
Juniper Green over Pine Green	Green, Grey, Stone or Tan
Marine Grey over Black	Blue, Green, Grey, Red, Stone or Tan
Marine Grey over Charcoal	Blue, Green, Grey, Red, Stone or Tan
Marine Grey over Light Navy	Blue, Grey or Stone
Marine Grey over Pine Green	Green, Grey, Stone or Tan
Steel Blue over Charcoal	Blue, Grey or Red
Steel Blue over Light Navy	Blue, Grey or Stone
Stone Grey over Burgundy	Grey, Red or Stone
Stone Grey over Juniper Green	Green, Grey, Stone or Tan
White over Marine Grey	Blue, Green, Red, Stone or Tan

Appendix D

Accessories

Rover always offered accessories, extras and options for the P4 range, and the table below is a comprehensive list of what was available and when. Some of the items listed as available from the start of production were in short supply or unavailable for several months afterwards because of raw materials shortages and manufacturing delays. Introduction dates should be seen as approximate, and of course items were often retro-fitted to older cars.

Badge bar	Available from the start. There were two types, one for the pre-1959 cars that mounted between the over-riders and one for the 1959 and later models that mounted to the number-plate box. This second type was not introduced until January 1961. The early type could not be fitted to the 90 or to other models with a foglamp.
Carburettor heater	This was intended only for the early 80 with the PAIO-5 carburettor, and was introduced in July 1961.
Cigarette lighter	Available from the start, and typically mounted alongside the heater control panel. It was standard on the 105S and 105R De Luxe. By late 1959, both Smith's and Magnatex types were supplied.
Compression plate	Available from the start for the 2,103-cc 75 engine, to lower the compression ratio to 6.50:1 to suit poor-quality petrol overseas.
Exhaust tailpipe finisher	This chrome finisher sleeve was available from January 1962.
Fitted suitcases	Two different types were available. Both were sets of three, sized and shaped to fit the P4's boot; one was made by Auto-Luggage Ltd of Barkingside in Essex. Several colours were available. These were not sold through Rover outlets.
Floor locker	Made by Nutilities of Birmingham and not available through Rover, this fitted to the transmission cover between the gear lever and the front seat. It was introduced in September 1963.
Floor mats	Available from the start. The early mats appear to have been solid black rubber types that were tailored to fit the front and rear footwells. Later ones, probably from autumn 1956, were link-type rubber mats.

Fog lamp	This became an option for the 1952 and later models and was mounted to the kerb side of the front bumper. It was standard on the 90 until the end of the 1956 season.
Foot rests	Available from the start, these were loose angled foot supports trimmed to match the carpets. They rested on the floor below the backs of the front seats.
Heated rear window	This was available as a production-line option only for the 95 and 110, and was embedded in the central pane of the rear window.
Immersion heater	This was available from April 1961 and was mostly fitted to models sent to cold-climate destinations overseas. It screwed into the cylinder block.
Individual seats	Individual front seats were optional from the start of the 1956 season but were never standard except on the 105S. Most had fixed backrests, but Lyback reclining seats were available for the 95 and 110.
Laminated windscreen	This was introduced as an option for the 95 and 110 but may have been fitted to some export models (e.g. for the USA) before that.
Overdrive	Overdrive was an option for the 1956–1958 90 and the 1957–1959 60 and 75; it was standard on the 105S and 105 and on the 1959 90, on the 80 and 100 (with exceptions) and on the 110.
Passenger foot rest	Available only for the Cyclops models, this was a loose angled foot support trimmed to match the carpets that rested in the passenger's front footwell.
Pillar pulls	Also known as 'dowager straps', these were available for the 80, 95 and 100, and standard on the 110.
Radio	Available from the start, the radio was normally mounted in the centre glovebox position. Early HMV types had a special mounting plate but others were often let into the wood of the glove box lid. Push-button types were supplied from the start of the 1957 season, initially by Radiomobile. A Pye set was initially approved for the 95 and 110 models, however customers frequently fitted their own choice of radio.
Radio aerial	In Britain, this was normally mounted to the roof above the centre of the windscreen. Wing-mounted aerials were preferred in some overseas territories.
Rear radio speaker	A radio speaker could be mounted in the rear parcels shelf on 95 and 110 models. It had a flush fit and a protective mesh grille.
Rear spring helper leaf	This was available for the 1957-season and later 90 models, and was intended for extreme conditions only.
Roof rack	Available from the start. This had a cream finish, rubber suction-cups on its feet, and was anchored to the drip rails.
Seat covers, felt	Available from the start, these were intended for hotter climates where the leather upholstery could be hot on a car that had been left standing in the sun.

Seat covers, Tygan	These were made of a patterned plastic material backed with cloth and were intended simply to protect the upholstery. They were introduced for the 1951 season, and various colours were available. They were not available for individual front seats.
Snow chains	Available from the start.
Spot lamp	A swivelling spot lamp manufactured by Lucas was available from July 1961.
Sunroof	The only sunroof approved by Rover was a Tudor Webasto fabric type that was made available for the 1964 season.
Sun visor, exterior	An exterior sun visor that mounted above the windscreen was available from the start of the 1955 season but was no longer advertised by the time of the 95 and 110. It was mainly fitted to counter strong sunlight in countries such as Africa and Australia.
Towbar	A towbar was available from the start. Some aftermarket types fouled the spare wheel door.
TV suppressor	Available from the start, this was not listed after mid-1954.
Two-tone paint	This was available from the start of the 1953 season.
Tyres	Wider 6.40 × 15 tyres became optional at the start of the 1959 season and remained so until the end; they were standard on 110 models.
Windscreen washer	This was optional on early 75 models from an unknown date and on the early 60, but became standard on the 1954-season and later 75 and 90, and on all later models.
Wheel trim rings	Available from the start, there were always two types. One was made by Ace ('Rimbellishers') and the other by Cornercroft. Rover supplied one type for the later 60, 75 and 90 (probably the Cornercroft type), and a different one for the 105S and 105R (probably the Ace type). The rings were standard on the 105, but could not be fitted to the 110.
Windtone horns	These were available on 1952 and later models, but were probably mainly used in the developing countries.
Wing mirrors	Available from the start, and normally fitted to the front wings. Door-mounted mirrors were favoured in some overseas countries.

This 1957 installation shows a push-button radio, with the speaker mounted above it.

Rarely seen in Britain, this is the external sun visor.

The fitted luggage set for the P4's boot was rare but very well made. The hydraulic struts supporting the boot lid are not an original feature.

Early radio installations typically had the head unit mounted into the lid of the centre glove box.

Early cars often had the speaker mounted above the windscreen. This one is in a 1950 model.

By 1953, a proper installation kit was available, and the speaker was mounted alongside the radio, which in this case is an HMV set.

The final type of radio installation is seen here, with a Radiomobile push-button set in a 110 that was sold in New Zealand.

Appendix E

UK Prices

Season	Model	Basic Price	Purchase Tax	Total
1950	75	£865	£241 0s 7d	£1,106 0s 7d
1951	75	£910	£253 10s 7d	£1,163 10s 7d
1952	75	£955	£532 1s 2d	£1,487 1s 2d
1953	75	£955	£532 1s 2d	£1,487 1s 2d
1954	60	£820	£342 15s 10d	£1,162 15s 10d
	75	£895	£374 0s 10d	£1,269 0s 10d
	90	£915	£382 7s 6d	£1,297 7s 6d
1955	60	£820	£342 15s 10d	£1,162 15s 10d
	75	£895	£374 0s 10d	£1,269 0s 10d
	90	£915	£382 7s 6d	£1,297 7s 6d
1956	60	£840	£351 2s 6d	£1,191 2s 6d
	75	£915	£382 7s 6d	£1,297 7s 6d
	90	£945	£394 17s 6d	£1,339 17s 6d
	90 (o/drive)	£990	£413 12s 6d	£1,403 12s 6d
1957	60	£865	£433 17s	£1,298 17s
	75	£943	£472 17s	£1,415 17s
	90	£976	£489 7s	£1,465 7s
	105S	£,1063	£532 17s	£1,595 17s
	105R	£1,099	£550 17s	£1,649 17s
	105R De Luxe	£1,130	£566 7s	£1,696 7s
1958	60	£883	£442 17s	£1,325 17s
	75	£963	£482 17s	£1,445 17s
	90 (Duo-tone)	£1,009	£505 17s	£1,514 17s
	105S	£1,088	£545 7s	£1,633 7s
	105R De Luxe (Duo-tone)	£1,165	£583 17s	£1,748 17s

Season	Model	Basic Price	Purchase Tax	Total
1959	60	£899	£450 17s	£1,349 17s
	75	£985	£493 17s	£1,478 17s
	90	£1,025	£513 17s	£1,538 17s
	105	£1,085	£543 17s	£1,628 17s
1960	80	£963	£402 7s 6d	£1,365 7s 6d
	100	£1,085	£453 4s 2d	£1,538 4s 2d
1961	80	£963	£402 7s 6d	£1,365 7s 6d
	100	£1,085	£453 4s 2d	£1,538 4s 2d
1962	80	£985	£452 13s 11d	£1,437 13s 11d
	100	£1,095	£503 2s 3d	£1,598 2s 3d
1963	95	£998	£375 5s 3d	£1,373 5s 3d
	110	£1,115	£419 2s 9d	£1,534 2s 9d
1964	95	£1,023	£213 13s 9d	£1,236 13s 9d
	110	£1,143	£238 13s 9d	£1,381 13s 9d